THE ULTIMATE
WEDDING

THE ULTIMATE WEDDING

CEREMONY
BOOK

By

By Bill Cox with Janie Franz

ISBN: 1-4196-8284-9
ISBN-13: 978-1419682841

CONTENTS

INTRODUCTION

You're engaged! Congratulations! There is so much to think about: a wedding dress, wedding colors, the rings, the flowers, the invitation list, the location, the vows, etc. Creating the perfect wedding can often be a stressful time with so many decisions to make while trying to please two families. Getting help from wedding professionals can simplify your life. These skilled resources are full of insider tips that can help you make economical and appropriate decisions. This book, written by a professional wedding dj and a seasoned wedding writer, brings over fifteen years' experience in the wedding industry to your fingertips.

The tried and true information found in this book can help you plan your perfect wedding. It is a companion book to the two others in the series: *The Ultimate Wedding Reception Book* and *The Ultimate Wedding Workbook*. This book, in particular, will guide you through every aspect of wedding ceremony planning. It covers everything you will need, whether you are a young, first-time bride or you are facing your second or even third marriage. It deals with budgeting, deciding on your wedding style, planning the ceremony, choosing a ceremony location, finding a wedding celebrant, defining the duties of your wedding party, choosing decorations and flowers, and even handling legal details. Also sprinkled throughout the book are tidbits about the origins of some of our favorite wedding traditions and customs. In addition, this book deals with a twenty-first century wedding trend: having the ceremony and the reception at the same location—and not necessarily at a church or synagogue.

Special chapters are devoted to planning the wedding ceremony itself. There are suggestions for selecting readings, prayers, and music. There are tips for writing your own vows and pointers for dealing with religious facilities, especially those with their own wedding planners. Also, included are ceremony extras like lighting a unity candle, recognizing parents and/or grandparents, and including children in your service.

Feel free to target special chapters that deal with your special wedding ceremony needs. And, please consult the list of wedding resources at the end of the book. They include books, websites, and sources for wedding services that will make your planning easier.

It is our wish that your wedding ceremony is the wedding of your dreams and that you approach your wedding day calmly and stress-free, knowing that all of the details are taken care of.

Blessings,

Bill Cox and Janie Franz

CHAPTER ONE

EARLY DECISIONS

Planning a wedding ceremony may seem like a daunting task. Even a small affair of twenty people has its own task list and order of events. That is one reason to enlist the help of other people, including the groom, your parents, and your bridesmaids and groomsmen. After all, that is the purpose of the wedding party today: to help the bride.

Though you are asking for assistance from your family and friends, you must remember that this is your wedding–yours and your groom's. Whatever decisions are made must make you both happy. By all means, accommodate some of each family's suggestions, but remember that you don't have to let Aunt Agnes sing at your wedding or hire the organist that Grandma likes, if you don't want to. Don't include anything that you feel you can't afford or don't feel comfortable doing. Create your own traditions through your own wedding planning.

This is critical if you are an encore bride, a bride whose wedding isn't her first. It's difficult enough to respect everyone's wishes when you are trying to accommodate two families (the bride's and the groom's), but it's impossible to accommodate the wishes of six or more families (the bride's parents who may be divorced and bringing new spouses, the groom's parents who may be divorced and bringing new spouses, the bride's children, the groom's children, the bride's in-laws who are her children's grandparents, and the groom's in-laws who are his children's grandparents—and maybe even the ex-spouses and their new husbands and wives). A remarriage today has become a tribal celebration, except that it is not confined to one small town but exists in a global community. By all means, include all of the people who are close to you. Just create a celebration that brings those people together to share your joy. After all, a wedding ceremony reflects the style and spirit of the couple who is being married.

Calendar and Timetable

Wedding ceremonies can be formal and/or reverent occasions. They can also be quite unusual, incorporating a non-traditional location or activity, such as a being married in a hot-air balloon. In any case, you will want to make sure you have enough time to complete any legal and/or religious obligations prior to your wedding, as well as schedule preparation for your wedding singers, musicians, and readers. In addition, you will need to plan for flowers, attire, ceremony location decorations, and a myriad of other delivery and service deadlines with wedding professionals. Planning ahead is the only way to get all of the decisions made and wedding services engaged and marked on calendars.

It's always better to plan as far ahead as you can, especially if the couple lives some distance from where they hope to celebrate their wedding. Many brides or grooms want to come home to their hometowns to be married, to share their celebration with old friends and to have the convenience of facilities closer to parents and relatives who might not be able to travel very far. In this instance, it might be helpful to enlist the aid of a wedding consultant/coordinator or a good friend who can help you do the legwork. And don't forget all of the technological conveniences: the Internet (for tracking down reception sites, florists, honeymoon destinations, even church planner guidelines, etc.), fax (for sending contracts back and forth), conference calling, etc.

Start planning as soon as possible. It's become common for couples to start planning a year and a half ahead of time. Part of the reason for that is the need to reserve the locations of the ceremony and the reception well in advance. A popular church, hall, or country club may not be available for the date you want if you don't reserve early and put down the necessary deposits.

Most of the wedding timetables in magazines or on-line suggest starting your planning six to twelve months ahead. The following timetable captures the entire wedding planning process, including planning the ceremony and the reception.

WEDDING TIME LINE

Nine to Twelve Months (or more)
> Select a wedding date and time
> Discuss financial obligations
> Decide on budget
> Decide on style of wedding (type and style)
> Select celebrant and attend initial meeting
> Choose location of ceremony and book the facility
> Schedule appointment with church/synagogue wedding consultants (if your religious facility requires one)
> Choose location of reception and book the facility
> Choose attendants
> Plan reception
> Select photographer/videographer
> Select caterer
> Select bridal registry
> Discuss honeymoon plans
> Reserve limousine transportation
> Start looking for florists
> Select gown, veil, & accessories, if you are special ordering or custom designing
> Draft initial guest lists

Six to Nine Months
> Select gown, veil, & accessories
> Select attendants' gowns

Select men's formalwear
Select music for ceremony
Book reception DJ or band
Compile guest lists (the bride's, the bride's family's, the groom's, the groom's family)
Order invitations
Reserve wedding night suite
Select florist and begin working on floral needs

Four to Six Months
Finalize honeymoon plans
Shop for trousseau
Find a new place to live
Shop for home furnishings
Set appointment for a physical exam and update your immunizations if you are going out of the country on your honeymoon
Find out the legal requirements for marriage in your state (when to apply for the license)
Set appointments for blood tests (if your state requires them)
Get passports if you are going out of the country
Help mothers select their dresses
Plan rehearsal dinner (Traditionally, the groom's parents does this.)
Register for gifts

Two to Four Months
Purchase wedding rings and have them engraved
Book accommodations for out-of-town guests
Book beauty appointments
Address invitations
Choose champagne and wines
Choose reception hall decor
Choose reception emcee

Check local newspapers about wedding announcement deadline

Reserve rental items necessary for the ceremony or reception

Order wedding and groom's cake

One to Two Months

Mail wedding invitations

Select attendants' gifts

Have a formal portrait taken in wedding gown for newspaper announcement

Purchase gifts for each other

Investigate legal details (changing beneficiaries, consolidating auto insurance, bank accounts)

Decide on a seating plan for the reception

Make arrangements to get foreign money for the honeymoon if you are going out of the country

Be sure attendants are informed of rehearsal plans, gown fittings, etc.

Arrange for final fitting of your gown

Confirm honeymoon trip reservations and check luggage

Test new hairstyles you may be considering

Arrange for ice sculptures for reception

Select reception music

Complete arrangements with photographer, florists, caterer, musicians/singers, DJ/band, reception hall, wedding celebrant

Write vows

Send copies of ceremony readings to wedding participants

Two Weeks

Follow up calls for invitations (unless your guests are very polite and they respond to RSVP's)

Record wedding gifts as you receive them and write thank-you notes promptly

Double check wedding attire and accessories for entire wedding party

Confirm time and date of wedding rehearsal with wedding party

Review reception seating plans and prepare place cards if necessary

Arrange to move your belongings to your new home

Select wedding announcements

One Week

Buy traveler's checks for honeymoon

Pack for honeymoon

Have a final consultation with caterer, florist, musicians/singers, DJ/band, MC, photographer/videographer, celebrant, reception hall, wedding ceremony site

Give final guest count to reception facility and caterer

Host bridesmaid's luncheon

Make sure that everyone arriving from out-of-town is met by someone, knows where everyone else is staying, etc.

Budget

Weddings can be very pricey. In 2005, the average wedding costs as much as a new car: $25,000. That average varies from region to region. In the Northeast, especially New York City, average wedding costs run around $42,000 to $50,000. Costs are less in the Southeast ($23,000), the Southwest ($23,000), and the Midwest ($26,000). First-rate events can run from $100,000 to a few million. An international model recently spent $35,000 on her wedding gown alone–much of that was for flying in two seamstresses to bead the dress.

Entertainment for the wedding reception can cost several thousand dollars, and catering and wedding cakes can also be pricey. When you add in wedding attire and accessories, church/hall fees, the celebrant's fee, flowers, decorations, gifts for attendants, invitations, etc., the total cost can easily approach that $25,000 average.

Today, parents of the bride don't always foot the bill for the wedding. Nearly 70% of all engaged couples pay for their own weddings, though sometimes the bride's parents and the groom's parents also contribute. It is appropriate to accept help from any family members (including grandparents or aunts and uncles), though they may want to underwrite a specific element in the wedding budget. For example, Uncle Harry wants to pay for the reception hall because he can reserve his union hall at a discount or Grandfather Smith has a green thumb and wants to provide flowers for the church. Even if relatives don't have special skills or discount connections, they may want to contribute to a general fund to pay for wedding expenses.

Setting up your wedding budget may not sound like the most fun thing to do since you've been dreaming about your wedding date, but that single act will shape every decision that you'll make from this point on. You may not want to decide on every little penny from the outset, but you will need to know what is the financial limit to your choices. If you want to keep costs down, there are several books available to help you plan your wedding on a tight budget. Most importantly, since you and your fiancé will pay for the wedding, you can feel freer to make your own choices and not feel so obligated to bow to the wishes of your families in areas that you don't want to.

Breakdown of Wedding Costs by Category For a $25,000 Budget		
Reception Reception site rental fee, food, tables, chairs, linens, wait-service, limo, misc. fees (40%) Alcohol and bartenders (10%) Cake (3%)	53% of total cost	$13,250
Bride's dress/accessories Gown, alterations, veil, train, undergarments, shoes (10%) Hairstyling and make-up (1%)	11%	$2,750
Music for ceremony and reception	9%	$2250
Photography/videography	8%	$2000
Ceremony and Rings Church/hall rental, celebrant's fee, wedding rings	7%	$1750
Flowers for ceremony and reception	7%	$1750
Stationery Invitations, postage, wedding programs, seating cards, thank you cards	4%	$1000
Groom's Attire	1%	$250

Of course, any of these categories can be adjusted according to your preferences. If you need to spend less in some areas, those might be in the flowers or invitations, or even the wedding gown itself. You can always adjust your reception costs, depending on what you are planning. For example, a friend might donate his ranch to host an outdoor reception or you could opt to serve fewer people. Some couples might want a wedding cake that looks like a piece of fine art whereas another couple wants a killer band for their reception. All of these different choices can be accommodated in any budget as long as you are willing to be flexible and trim costs somewhere else.

Wedding Expense Responsibilities

Traditionally, wedding expenses have been allotted to each family and to the bride and groom. The bride pays for the groom's ring and his gift, her attendant's gifts, and lodging for out-of-town bridesmaids. The groom pays for the bride's rings and her wedding gift, the gifts for the groomsmen and Best Man, the marriage license, the celebrant's fee, flowers for the mothers and grandmothers, boutonnieres for the Best Man and groomsmen, the bride's bouquet and going-away corsage, lodging for out-of-town groomsmen, and the honeymoon expenses.

The groom's family takes care of their own wedding attire, their travel expenses, their lodging, a wedding gift for the bridal couple, and the rehearsal dinner. The groomsmen and the Best Man pay for their own attire, transportation for the wedding party, wedding gifts for the couple, and valet parking. The bride's attendant's pay for their own gowns and accessories, their travel expenses, and a wedding gift for the bride and groom. The bride's family pays for everything else.

Size

There are two very important initial decisions you will need to make regarding your budget. How big do you want the wedding to be, and what kind of wedding do you want?

Size of the wedding is usually determined in general first. Do you want a small, intimate wedding with just your parents and some very close friends? Or, do you want to invite your entire hometown and celebrate for hours? That decision will set the tone for the wedding style you will choose. It also will help shape your budget. A small, intimate wedding and reception naturally will not cost as much as a pull-out-all-the-stops wedding at the biggest church in town and a reception and dance at the local country club.

Size, however, may change once you start comparing your guest lists with your parents' lists. Try to only invite people you care about the most and who have been involved with your life. Just remember, though, that each added guest will create additional costs for the reception in food and drink and perhaps extra seating and tables, especially if you are renting them. More guests may also mean that you may need to move the wedding or the reception to a larger facility.

Invitation Lists

When you first begin thinking about your wedding, you and your groom will toss out names of people you would like to invite to your wedding. At first, that list will be quite modest, composed mainly of your immediate families and your best friends. Soon, however, you will begin to remember people who invited you to their weddings, old family friends, aunts and uncles, and business associates. Your parents will also be thinking of people that they will feel obligated to invite as well. That is one reason why there should be three working invitation lists at first.

On the first go around on the bridal couple's invitation list, brainstorm everyone you can think of that you'd want to invite. Count the number of guests you have. Have each set of parents write down their choices and count up the number of their guests.

Then, collect the three lists and merge them together into one working list, but save the original lists so that you can negotiate with each group of list makers. Eliminate duplicate names and count the number of guests you now have all together. You will probably find that you have too many guests for your budget or for the size of wedding you had envisioned. Don't panic. This is the time to pare down each individual list, well before emotions start to heat up.

Send the lists back to each set of parents and ask them to trim the lists down to the most important people they want to invite. Remind everyone that each guest will increase your wedding costs. Do the same with your own list. Then, combine the lists once more and count up the number of guests. The numbers should be now within your original concept. If the numbers are not, purge once more. Keep doing it until you have the number you can afford. If there are still a few too many, juggle your budge to accommodate this number or ask for additional help from your families, especially if the extra numbers are guests you don't really know.

Bridal Registry

Bridal Registries are very helpful for bridal couples. They aren't just wish lists for greedy brides and grooms. They have become essential for families and friends to find the perfect gifts for the bridal couple at reasonable prices, especially if they live out of town. Today, you can register at most large department stores and even large discount stores. These lists are available on line so that your family and friends can get what you need in the style you want at a price they can afford. The registry lists are updated when you purchase items at the stores and can be updated by the couple even if someone bought something from another retail outlet.

Legal and Religious Obligations

Check with your county or state for legal requirements for your marriage. Determine when marriage licenses need to be filled out and how long they are legal. Some are good for six months; others, much less. Determine also whether you need blood tests or marriage classes. Some states offer a discount on the marriage license if the couple takes pre-marriage training. In addition, schedule an appointment with a lawyer if you will be drawing up a pre-nuptial agreement.

Discuss you wedding plans with the celebrant of your choice and meet with the facility's wedding planner, if the church or synagogue has one. Find out the facility's timeline and requirements. Schedule any marriage classes or counseling that the celebrant or church requires.

CHAPTER TWO

KEEPING IT LEGAL

Marriage License

One of the first things a couple needs to check out is how to make the marriage legal. To do that, you will need a marriage license. State and county regulations vary. Determine when marriage licenses need to be filled out and how long they are legal. Some are good for six months; others, much less.

Determine also whether you will need blood tests or marriage classes. Some states offer a discount on the marriage license if the couple takes pre-marriage training. This could take some time since some pre-marriage classes may last up to six months. This requirement must be completed before applying for the marriage license.

Once you know what your state or county requires, then you can rough out the wedding date. Discuss your wedding plans with the celebrant you have chosen. If you are being married in a church or synagogue, meet with the facility's wedding planner, if the church or synagogue has one, and look over the physical layout of the space. See if it will fit the size of your wedding ceremony. Also, look at the church or synagogue's social hall to see if it is suitable for your wedding. If you will be getting married in some other location and/ or will be having your reception somewhere else, check out a few possible locations. Find out whether each facility has your wedding date open and what their timeline is and their requirements are. You may need to adjust your wedding date once you have a facility chosen.

Once the wedding date is determined, you can then schedule when to go to the courthouse to fill out the necessary paperwork for your marriage license.

Name Change Options

In the twenty-first century, brides aren't bound by social custom to take their husband's last name, though many women still do. In the past, when Nancy Wilson married Justin Davis, she became Mrs. Justin Davis and was forever known as Mrs. Davis. (If she divorced, she became Mrs. Nancy Davis to indicate her changed marital status. That custom no longer applies today.) Today, a new bride who takes her husband's surname is called Mrs. Nancy Davis or just Nancy Davis.

Some women feel that taking their husband's name diminishes them and choose to keep their maiden names. Other women keep their maiden names for professional reasons. For example, if Nancy Wilson were a lawyer or a doctor, she might continue to be known as Nancy Wilson or Dr. Nancy Wilson. This name choice does not identify a woman's marital status. Many women feel that it isn't necessary to do this since men historically haven't had to broadcast whether they were married or not.

Another option for brides who want to keep some connection with their family surname choose to use it as a middle name or to hyphenate it with their husband's last name. Nancy Wilson would become Nancy Wilson Davis or Nancy Wilson-Davis. This option is ideal for the woman who is an only child or is the only namesake to her father's family name. She will need to remember to use her full name when stating who she is. The couple's children may either take the hyphenated name or take their father's name. Some women feel that hyphenation makes the last name too long and makes the name harder to say.

Some couples take each other's last names as middle names. Nancy Wilson would be Nancy Davis Wilson and Justin Davis would become Justin Wilson Davis. This could become confusing for genealogical records, but it honors both families and keeps the romance of trading names.

For the twenty-first century, other couples have been choosing to step into a fresh, new name choice. They are deciding to hyphenate both the bride's name and the groom's name. Nancy and her husband Justin become Nancy Wilson-Davis and Justin Wilson-Davis. And some men are even taking their bride's last name, just as the bride would have taken the groom's. State laws vary about this practice, but a number of states are bowing to this growing custom.

More adventurous couples are choosing an entirely different name. Some couples blend their last names. For example, the Wilson and Davis names could become Dason or Wilvis. Others pick a name that has some significance during their courtship. A favorite restaurant or location could become their surname of choice. For example, if they met or spent their dates in Las Vegas, they may choose to be Mr. and Mrs. Vegas. Again, state laws vary about this.

Finally, some brides use their maiden names in their profession or in the workplace, but actually take their husband's name legally. A problem with this occurs if the woman needs to show identification showing her maiden name in the workplace.

When to Make the Change

Just saying, "I do," doesn't change your name. Legal name changes normally occur after the wedding when the official marriage license is sent to the couple. Then, the bride can use the marriage license to verify the name change. Because there is a delay, this can complicate honeymoon plans since most airlines and customs officials need to have all travel documents bearing a consistent name. Though Nancy Wilson-Davis is legally married, none of her identification will reflect that a few hours after the wedding. Nancy will need to travel under her maiden name, with airline tickets, credit cards, and passport bearing the name Nancy Wilson. She and Justin can freely sign the hotel registry as Mr. and Mrs. since the couple is usually given a keepsake marriage license after the wedding. Even if the wedding celebrant doesn't offer one, the couple shouldn't feel shy about claiming their marital status at the hotel.

When you return from your honeymoon, you can start filling out papers and calling insurance and credit card companies. In some cases, the county or state Supreme Court will authorize a legal name change after you file a Petition for Change of Name. In this case, you will need to show your birth certificate and your marriage license when you file the petition. Most of these are done either through your lawyer or through a county or state court office.

Documents to Change

Though this may be the electronic age, we still are faced with so much paperwork. All of it will need to show your legal name change and/or your change of address. Try to make both of these changes together and as soon after your honeymoon as possible. If you send any name changes by mail, send them by registered mail and include a return receipt request. This assures that your name change documentation gets into the proper hands.

Social Security Card. The first legal name change you should make is your Social Security card. This name change will help you with other legal documents. Go to your Social Security office with your driver's license, your marriage license, and our old Social Security card. Changing your name there is free.

Driver's License. You can either call your local Department of Motor Vehicles (DMV) or search for its website to find out what forms of identification you will need to bring with you to the DMV office. Usually, it's your current driver's license and your marriage certificate.

Include your change of address at the same time. These changes are usually made while you wait as when you get your driver's license renewed. There is usually a small fee.

Passport. This name change takes longer, usually about six weeks. You can pick up name change request forms where you obtained your passport originally. Usually, you send in the request form, your old passport, a copy of your marriage certificate, and the necessary fee to the U.S. State Department's Passport Center in Charleston, SC. There your married name will be stamped on the last page of your original passport. You can speed up the process by shipping everything by two-day mail and including return postage. This usually takes only about a week.

Credit Cards, Bank Accounts, Checks. These changes should be made as soon as possible. Some of them can be begun before the wedding ceremony takes place. Go to your bank and talk with your customer service representative about changing the names on your checks and other bank accounts. Your bank signature cards may need to be signed after you return from your honeymoon, but checks can be ordered as close to the wedding as you can in order to have them available for your use after your wedding trip. Paperwork for joint checking accounts is usually completed after the wedding ceremony. (One caution: Don't put your social security numbers on your checks.)
Call your credit card companies about your name change and ask what documentation is needed. Then send each company a letter with copies of the necessary identification papers.

Frequent Flyer Accounts. If you want to keep your frequent flyer miles, you'll need to have your name changed on your frequent flyer account. Find out where to send your documentation from the airlines website. Email or call the airlines to find out how to make a name change. Usually, you will need to send them a copy of your marriage license, your member number, and a copy of your travel itinerary showing your honeymoon location, if you flew there under your maiden name. This verifies credit for your honeymoon miles.

Post Office. Just before the wedding or as soon after you return from your honeymoon, go to the post office and fill out change of address and/or change of name forms. This is a free service.

Other Legal Changes

When you get married, a number of other papers and lists will need to be changes. Often couples add their spouses to their medical insurance policies at work. They change their life insurance beneficiaries to their spouses. Jointly owned property such as homes and automobiles are often changed to reflect both spouses.

Women also need to remember to change their names on stocks and mutual funds. They need to change their names on voter registration rolls. In addition, all medical and dental records will need to be changed, as well as employee records and even magazine subscriptions, clubs, gyms, schools, and alumni associations. Car titles and deeds will need to be changed also. Utilities, telephone contracts, and Internet services should be changed as well. Finally, wills and advanced directives will need to reflect your name change and changes in beneficiaries. Medical powers of attorney can be changed to the new spouse.

Prenuptial Agreements

Some couples, especially those with lots of assets, may choose to have a prenuptial agreement. These documents protect the spouse who has the most assets from marrying someone who just is interested in inheriting money or property. These agreements can be very lean, stating that the poorer spouse will not receive anything upon the other's death or divorce, to very generous, detailing just how much of a settlement the wealthier spouse will grant the other at death or divorce. In most cases, these agreements are made by people who are very wealthy or are celebrities. However, some are drawn up by older couples that have accumulated a modest estate and want to pass it on to their children and not to their spouses.

Schedule an appointment with a lawyer to discuss your wishes. The lawyer will draft the pre-nuptial agreement, and both spouses will need to sign it.

Insurance

Many couples are opting to include insurance in their wedding planning. A recent concept in the United States, wedding insurance has been commonplace in Great Britain. It has taken root here because of the growing litigious nature of this country. If someone falls at your wedding dance and receives an injury and if the site doesn't have liability insurance, you will be responsible for any lawsuits as a result of the accident. You might wish to look at limited liability insurance for your wedding.

Wedding cancellations or postponements due to illness or injury of a member of the wedding party or because of airport closings due to bad weather are typical wedding insurance policy coverage. Since weddings are very expensive affairs, involving a team of vendors and professionals, wedding insurance can help recoup losses if your wedding is postponed or cancelled for any number of reasons, including weather emergencies or military service.

Most wedding insurance policies range from $155 to $385 for a $50,000 policy for cancellation alone. Though most venues (churches, halls, restaurants, country clubs, etc.) have liability insurance, purchasing your own insurance policy in case of accident or injury may be a good move. If you are planning on having your wedding at your family's home, for example, you should look over the homeowner's policy liability limits. Many policies won't cover special events for large groups of people like weddings. Therefore, a separate liability policy is essential. It may also be required if you plan to rent space at an historic building or mansion, vineyard, or park.

CHAPTER THREE

WEDDING PANACHE: FINDING YOUR WEDDING STYLE

Wedding Style

Once you determine the size of your wedding and reception, then you are ready to look at your wedding style. Finding your style means looking at the type of wedding you want and deciding on a theme for your wedding.

Time of Day

There are two concerns when deciding on a wedding type. The first is the time of day you want to have your wedding and reception. In America today, you can get married at almost any time of day or night, on any day of the week. The only constraints are those of availability of the wedding facilities and the celebrant, and the flexibility of your guests. It is perfectly OK to have a wedding and reception in the morning, at noon, at teatime, in the evening, or even at midnight. Sometimes you can have the wedding at one time of day and the reception at another.

Some couples choose morning weddings with a breakfast or brunch reception. Sometimes couples want to view the morning light at a specific place, or they want to get married and then catch an early plane to their honeymoon destination. Others just want to start the day married and then be able to carry out a series of festivities throughout the rest of the day. Still others find a brunch less expensive than an evening buffet and dance. Regular breakfast fare is served along with wedding cake and lots of hot coffee and tea. Champagne and champagne punch may also be served.

Luncheon receptions usually follow an 11:00 or noon wedding. A buffet or sit-down meal is served between 12:00 and 2 pm. If a hall is rented, a wedding dance can follow, with guests leaving no later than about 4 pm. Reception menus for luncheons are very similar to evening receptions, except the portions may be smaller. It is very acceptable to provide champagne at a luncheon reception, and bar service may be served as well.

A tea or cocktail reception comes after an early afternoon wedding. The tea reception is usually served between 2 pm and 5 pm. Tea sandwiches and finger foods are served with coffee and tea, of course. A champagne punch may also be served. This is the least expensive reception to provide. You can entertain a large number of guests with a small amount of cash.

The cocktail reception is served later, between 4 pm and 7:30 pm. Wine, beer, and champagne punch are offered with hot and cold hors d'oeuvres. Bar service also may be provided. You can also offer music for dancing or ambiance here as well as at the tea reception.

The most common reception type is the evening reception with a dinner served either sit-down or as a buffet. This is also the most costly due to the fact that you are providing a complete meal, liquor, and usually a dance band or a DJ for entertainment. Catering, decorating, liquor choices, the wedding cake, and entertainment are the most costly expenditures. These are also areas where you can try to trim costs.

Formality

The second question you must answer when determining wedding type is the degree of formality you want at your wedding and reception. It is usually not cool to mix very formal with informal. Though size is usually the first indicator of formal or informal type of reception, you can have a very large informal gathering and you can have a small, intimate, very formal affair.

Very Formal. Usually, formal events are very large, serving over 200 people. The ceremony and/or reception location is elegant: a country club, a ballroom, an historic estate, or a museum. The bride is dressed in a traditional gown with a chapel or cathedral length train (shorter during the day). Between four and twelve bridesmaids wear floor-length gowns. Groom and groomsmen wear white tie and tails for an evening wedding or cutaway coats for the daytime. A live band usually plays the wedding dance. Flowers and decorations are elegant. Tables are dressed with fine linens and china, silver, and crystal. Chairs often have slipcovers in the bride's colors or the colors of the wedding theme.

Formal. This type of wedding is very similar to the very formal, except it's for a smaller crowd, usually over 100 guests. The reception site can be a church hall, hotel ballroom, club, or home. The bride wears a long gown with a chapel, sweep, or detachable train. She may wear a shorter gown if the wedding is scheduled during the day. Her attendants (two to six) can wear either short or long dresses. The groom and his men wear gray strollers, waistcoats, striped trousers and ties for day or black tuxedos for evening. Again, a sit-down reception is usually served, although a formal tea or cocktail reception can be offered. A jazz combo or string quartet can provide ambience, depending on your theme. You can also have a wedding dance.

Semi-formal. Again, this is similar to formal but a tad folksier for a group of less than 100 people. The ceremony and reception locations can be either indoors or outdoors, at a beach or park, a private home, hotel, church hall, or banquet facility. The bride can wear whatever length gown she wants in whatever color she wants. She can have a short or long veil. Her attendants (between one and three) can wear whatever they wish also. The groom and groomsmen usually wear suits and ties for a day wedding and tuxedos or dinner jackets for an evening one. A buffet is usually served instead of a sit-down dinner. Music can be either a band or DJ.

Informal. Here the wedding is for a small intimate group, usually less than 50. The reception can be outside or at a home or restaurant. The bride can wear a suit or dress in whatever color she wants. There is usually only one attendant who wears a suit or short dress. The groom and best man wear suits or blazers with slacks. Music can also be a live band or DJ or it can be a single performer.

These degrees of formality are generalities. There have been quite tasteful weddings that have bent these rules. If you want fewer attendants at your formal wedding, you can do that. If you want more at your very informal wedding, you can do that, too. You can do whatever you want at your wedding as long as your guests are prepared for it.

Personality

One other consideration about type is really a reflection on your personality. Are you a traditional person or a non-traditional person? Your wedding can reflect either. The following profiles are examples of the traditional, traditional with flair, and non-traditional personalities.

Traditional Personality

You are interested in following what Ms. Manners says.
You plan your wedding according to a classic wedding planner.
You want to be introduced at the reception as Mr. & Mrs.
You want to wear your mother's wedding gown.
You want your reception to be a formal sit-down dinner.
You thought Lady Di's wedding was the model for the perfect
  wedding.

Traditional with a Flair Personality

A theme wedding sounds like fun but you want to keep it
  tasteful.
You want to be introduced as, "John Smith and Mary Jones-
Smith."
You want to write your own vows.
You do everything the wedding books say, but you do it your
  way.
You'd rather get married in a pastel color or a white dress that
  fits your theme.

Nontraditional Personality

The idea of a big, formal wedding makes you sweat.
You want something totally out of the ordinary–like skydiving.
You want to write your own wedding ceremony.
You really want to hire a zydeco band and serve Cajun food.
You don't want to register for gifts.
A barefoot beach wedding is appealing to you.
You want to be introduced as, "John Smith and Mary Jones."
You want your wedding and reception to be something that your friends and family
will talk about for years.
You want to be married in any color except white or ivory.
Your wedding rings will be designed by an artist that you know personally.
You want to be married at Disneyland.
You want to be introduced as, "John and Mary Smith-Jones."
The wedding band is the group you and your fiancé toured with last summer.

Theme

Theme weddings may naturally form out of special circumstances. For example, you or your fiancé are members of the military. It would only be natural to have a military wedding with all of the trimmings reflecting that. Other themes come from your family backgrounds, interests, or dreams.

Ethnic Themes. Another natural theme is one of ethnicity. For example, if you are Asian, you might want to be married in red and decorate your reception hall with traditional colors or decorations that reflect your heritage. Almost any ethnic or cultural background could be brought into a wedding theme.

There are new wedding books and wedding consultants who specialize in Irish weddings, Polish weddings, Greek weddings, or African-American weddings.

Cultural Themes. A form of the ethnic theme is the cultural wedding. This can be a luau, a fiesta, a New England clambake, a western barbeque, Octoberfest, or even a Mardi Gras theme. If you are marrying in the West or in a rural area (or you just like the theme), you might want to do a western wedding or a country wedding, complete with a horse and buggy in lieu of a limousine.

Fantasy Themes. Closely related to the cultural themes are fantasy themes. Roman or Egyptian theme weddings might cross into the fantasy realm when the couple doesn't have a connection with the culture. For example, an Egyptian theme might be more of a cultural theme for two archaeology students, but would be a fantasy theme for someone else.
Some couples have had unusual fantasy themes, such as a clown theme wedding, an African safari theme, a carousel theme, or a cruise ship theme. Some have even drawn their wedding theme from their honeymoon destination. For example, the couple could set up a Polynesian or rain forest theme if they are honeymooning in the South Pacific or in Rio de Janeiro. Some couples have also chosen movie themes such as an Indiana Jones theme, a Star Trek or Star Wars theme, or just the glamour of Hollywood. And, some have created Lord of the Rings and other elven fantasy themes, complete with cloaks and fairy wings.

Period Themes. Some couples want to recapture a time long ago, either because they are members of a re-creationist group like SCA, the Society for Creative Anachronism, or because they just thought a specific time period was special. SCA weddings are medieval, courtly weddings with knights and ladies. There is information on the Internet and in some publications on just how to create a medieval wedding. They offer authentic advice about wedding attire and even the wedding feast, which, in those times, was a many-course affair that went on for hours. These feasts often are prepared by SCA members who have special skills in catering these affairs, and they are well worth the time to cultivate their acquaintance. The food is definitely worth it!

Some of the more accessible themes that couples have tried have revolved around other time periods. A Big Band wedding would capture the feel of the 1940's. The bride might wear an antique gown or a copy and long, over-the-elbow gloves. The reception, of course, would have a full, swing orchestra with lots of champagne flowing.

Other time periods could be a Roaring Twenties wedding, a Victorian wedding, a Renaissance wedding, a Southern plantation wedding, or even a Fifties wedding. These aren't silly, over-the-top ideas. They can be pulled off tastefully or with as much impishness as you can muster. Most of these period themes deal with specific types of dress: brocades and velvets for a Renaissance wedding; high-necked, lace gowns or wispy, angelic chiffons for a Victorian wedding; hoopskirts and parasols for a Southern plantation wedding; strings of pearls and lace smocking for a Roaring Twenties wedding; and even full-skirted, pinch-waisted gowns for a Fifties wedding.

Some of these themes would be perfect at specific locations. For instance, a Southern plantation wedding could be held at a park, a formal garden, a museum, or a turn-of-the-century hall or country club. A Victorian wedding might be great at an historic building, a garden, or a castle.

Outdoor and Recreation Themes. These weddings can be formal ones that are held outside under trees or a canvas canopy. Seaside or beach weddings fall into this category. Garden weddings, either in your grandmother's spacious backyard or a public English rose garden, are other kinds of outdoor weddings. Weddings at historical sites often require special permission well in advance, but they can be pulled off.

Recreation theme weddings can be anything that the couple and the wedding guests enjoy. Skiing, skydiving, and scuba weddings have been performed. These unusual weddings are mostly small with sometimes only the bridal couple and the celebrant engaging in the activity while the guests watch and greet the couple when the ceremony is finished. Camping, sports, or other types of recreation themes can involve the wedding party and guests, but they sometimes take a lot of planning. Some couples have been married at half time during a football game or on the pitcher's mound before a baseball game. These locations would require special permission of the facility as well as the teams involved.

Amusement Park Themes. One really popular wedding theme is the vacation resort or amusement park theme. These weddings actually take place at a vacation resort or amusement park. Disneyland and Walt Disney World both have wedding planners to create the ideal Fairy Tale wedding. They provide everything from catering, flowers, makeup artists, photographers, and the perfect wedding cake. You can also ride in Cinderella's Glass Coach for an extra fee.

SeaWorld, Knott's Berry Farm, Busch Gardens, and Opryland all have wedding packages. Knott's Berry Farm even offers art deco decorations and ice sculptures. SeaWorld throws in the flowers and a harpist. You can also have a sea lion act as ring bearer. Busch Gardens presents an elegant wedding with hors d'oeuvres, fine wines and champagnes, dinner, flowers, and entertainment–all at the Crown Colonial House. These theme park weddings provide everything–for a price. Usually, if you only want your parents to witness your wedding, or just your best man and maid of honor, these packages are affordable. They can be cost prohibitive for large weddings, however, if you are paying for them. They can also be burdensome for your guests if they have to pay for travel and park admission themselves.

Destination Wedding. A version of the amusement park theme is the destination wedding that combines the honeymoon location with the ceremony. There are wedding consultants in exotic places like Bermuda or Jamaica who handle all of the details for your out-of-the-country wedding. You can legally be married in another country, have the event photographed, enjoy a fine dinner afterwards, and sometimes have a few days at a resort thrown in–all for a flat fee.

Seasonal and Holiday Themes. Another type of theme wedding theme is the seasonal or holiday wedding. Autumn harvest, Christmas, Valentine's Day, or winter themes take their colors and decorations from the season. For an Easter wedding, some couples have even hidden colored Easter eggs around the reception site and given their guests baskets to collect them in.

Sometimes, a period, cultural, ethnic, or fantasy wedding can also have the decorations or colors of a holiday or season. For example, a fairy and elves wedding could have oak leaves and acorns as decoration elements if the wedding is held in the fall or it could have snowflakes and white flowers for a winter wedding.

Traditional Wedding Themes. Traditional wedding decorations have sometimes been used as themes in themselves. For example, a couple could have hearts, doves, or candles as the main decoration theme for a formal, traditional wedding. Other themes might revolve around the bold use of your wedding colors.

CHAPTER FOUR

ENCORE COUPLES

Encore Couples

An encore bride or groom is a person who is not marrying for first time. The intended spouse may have been married before also, or this may be a first wedding. Because it is a remarriage, plan carefully and don't make it a second-best wedding.

One of the first things a mother and father who have been married before should do is quietly discuss their engagement with their children. This should be done privately on a mom to children or dad to children basis. Take time to answer all of your children's questions. Sometimes, children feel that a wedding dashes any hopes of their parents ever reconciling so it may take some time for children to accept the inevitability of the marriage and see its positive side.

Ask your children if they would like to be part of the wedding. In many cases, child psychologists have found that children feel disconnected to the remarrying parent if they are not included in the wedding. To get a phone call or receive a picture of Dad and his new wife can be devastating, especially if the children have not gotten to know their stepmother or don't like her. Participating in the wedding can be therapeutic. At no point, however, should you force the child to be part of the wedding if the child just can't do it. Please do invite the reluctant child to the wedding and try to give him or her some of your precious time on the day of the wedding.

Next, the encore bride and groom should tell their own parents and then their ex-spouses. When the children are told and they live with the ex-spouse, that is a good time to tell the ex-spouse because he or she will learn the news from the children anyway. Reactions will vary, depending on the amicability of the divorce.

Ex-in-laws may be invited if they wish to see their grandchildren participate in the wedding ceremony. Sometimes, though, ex-in-laws bear a grudge longer and harder than ex-spouses and may find an invitation to your remarriage hard to take. Use your judgment about extending them invitations.

If the encore bride and groom have lost a spouse through death, a remarriage is often a time for ex-in-laws to put aside grief. They should be invited.

As stated previously, only invite those who will share your joy on your wedding day. Encore couples really have the luxury of creating healthy boundaries because they usually don't have parents who will insist, this time, to invite all of their relatives or their business associates. You can invite your own business associates and anyone else who will make your day happy.

Couples with Children

Because encore brides are blending families, you may choose to include family members in your ceremony. Traditionally, having children at a wedding or in a wedding celebration has been considered to be good luck. Include them, if you wish, but remember to assign them duties that are age-appropriate and fit their personalities. An active little girl might hate being a flower girl and standing still throughout the wedding. But she might love talking to people at the wedding book and encouraging them to sign it. Children's attention spans are brief, and they can get restless when they have to sit or stand for long periods. They also always seem to need to eat all of the time. So, if you can, please feed the children as soon as possible, perhaps a light, non-drippy snack just before the ceremony. Please remember, also, that formal photos should include the children in the wedding party first so that they can be dismissed to get food at the reception or go outside and play. These photo sessions should be brief.

And, please, remember that children, like adults, need to preserve their own dignity at any cost. Make sure that what events you create for children have the children's best interests in mind.

Children, grown or young, might become members of the wedding party. Some daughters have been bridesmaids or even the maid of honor, but only if she is able to perform those duties during the wedding ceremony. Another bridesmaid could handle much of the legwork that a maid or matron of honor does. You might choose a child to read something special or sing or play a musical selection.

For some brides, their fathers have passed away and cannot walk down the aisle with them again. These brides can ask a stepfather, uncle, or family friend to do so. Some have just forgone that tradition and come down the aisle alone. Other brides have chosen not to have their fathers walk down the aisle with them. Instead, they ask their eldest son to do those honors. Some have even asked their daughters to do this. Furthermore, some fathers have asked their sons to be their best men.

In some cases, encore brides have walked down the aisle with all of their children. The encore groom stands at the front with his children and his groomsmen. Some children have also stood with their parents while the vows were being said as a way to affirm the blending of two families.

If there are children on both sides of the new marriage, try to involve them together in some of the planning. Crafts such as making wedding favors, banners, and table decorations are good group activities for children to get to know each other and begin to feel like step brothers and sisters. This is especially important if all of the children will be living in the encore couple's new home.

Prenuptial Agreements

Encore couples find that prenuptial agreements can save them a lot of headaches, especially after they found out the hard way how difficult it was to dissolve a marriage once before. Also called ante nuptial agreements, these documents are essential if either the bride or the groom has a lot of assets, a high income, or will inherit a lot of money in the future. Prenuptial agreements detail terms for the possession of all of the assets, how future income will be treated, who controls individual property, and how their assets will be divided in case of divorce.

This is especially important for couples with children in order to provide for their future. Prenuptial agreements protect money that each spouse may have saved for their children's education or for their own retirement before the marriage. It also details what the children's property rights are and how they'll be supported during their parent's marriage and later in case of divorce or death.

Each spouse should have a lawyer draw up a prenuptial agreement and then meet to combine both documents into one that is satisfactory to the encore bride and groom. This document declares all assets, determines what is jointly owned and what is owned separately, the division of the property upon divorce, inheritance of the property, and spousal support obligations. These are necessary decisions that the couple must make, and deciding them before the marriage lays everything out in the open.

A trip to your lawyer's office, your insurance agent, and your financial planner will save you headaches later on. Get wills and beneficiaries changed. It is estimated that 83% of people divorce because these decisions weren't discussed before couples married.

CHAPTER FIVE

WHO'S WHO: WEDDING PARTY

Origins of the Wedding Party

There are two stories that illustrate how the wedding party may have come about. In ancient Egypt, it was thought, weddings attracted evil spirits who wanted to spoil the joyous occasion. In order to confuse the evil spirits and to protect the bride, several women from the bride's family dressed exactly like the bride and accompanied the bride to the wedding. The bride also carried a bouquet of scented herbs and flowers to help ward off bad spirits.

The other story says that the origins of the bridal party was in medieval times when a young man saw a young lady that he wanted for his wife and carried her off to his home or to the church. The women in the bride's family would gather around her and protect her from the groom. Later, they began to dress exactly like the bride in order to confuse him. The groom also brought his best friend to help fight off the maiden's brothers. As brides began to collect more female helpers, grooms also brought more friends to help them. Both the bride and the groom eventually had groups of family and friends surrounding them, all dressed similarly. The women also began wearing veils to confuse the groom further. This tradition continued into Victorian England. Soon, the bridal abduction became a high-spirited tradition that was part of a more formal ceremony and celebration.

The groom also put the bride on his left side so that he could use his sword hand to fend off the bride's family. That is why the bride is on the left in most wedding ceremonies.

How Many?

Determining the size of your wedding party can be tricky, especially if you are being pressured by your parents to include family members or family friends. You will need to remember that wedding party size is a reflection of the size of the wedding. A large 200-person affair can accommodate a large wedding party. A smaller wedding naturally would have a smaller wedding party. Your personal style also helps determine just how many to include. Usually, the bride and the groom try to have the same number of attendants each so that both sides will look balanced. If either the bride or the groom has fewer friends or relatives, that will also be a factor in settling on the size of the wedding party.

If you are an encore bride, you don't have to ask the same people to be in your wedding party as before. Time has passed, and you have changed. Maybe you have even lost touch with the people in your wedding, especially if you or they have moved. It is perfectly all right to ask new people to be part of your new wedding.

Duties of the Best Man

The best man is the groom's right hand during the wedding planning, the ceremony, and the reception. He should be close to the groom and be very trustworthy. Choosing your college dorm mate who was always late for class and got drunk every chance he got may not be the best choice for best man. He has heavy responsibilities.

The best man helps the groom find accommodations for out-of-town ushers and groomsmen. He helps the groom dress for the ceremony and holds the wedding ring until called for at the ceremony. As one of the two mandatory witnesses, he signs the marriage license and gives the celebrant his fee (from the groom, usually in a sealed envelope). The best man sits on the bride's right at the reception, dances with the maid/matron of honor during the first dance, and offers the first toast. He gathers the single men for the garter toss during the reception.

The best man attends pre-wedding parties, the rehearsal, and the rehearsal dinner. He organizes the bachelor party.

After the reception, he helps the groom change into his going away clothes and makes sure the bridal couple's luggage is placed in the get-away transportation. He arranges for that transportation or drives the bridal couple to the airport or hotel himself. He and the maid/matron of honor gather the wedding gifts and bring them to the bride and groom's home. He collects all of the rented formalwear from the groomsmen and the groom and returns them to the rental store on time.

The best man pays for his clothing, his travel expenses, wedding gifts for the couple, and contributes toward valet parking at the reception. He may also share the expense of the bachelor party with the other groomsmen.

On some rare occasions, the groom's best man is a woman, often dressed in a tuxedo to match the other groomsmen. It is unusual, but if the groom feels strongly about having a female best man, there is nothing to stop him from doing so. In these cases, the woman is a long-time friend and has a sisterly relationship with the groom. (Traditionally, friends like these or the groom's sisters or cousins are included as bridesmaids.) Sometimes, a woman stands up with the groom because there isn't anyone else to do so.

Fathers and sons have even stood as a groom's best man. Usually, it is a brother or best friend.

Duties of the Maid/matron of Honor

Like the best man, the maid/matron of honor must be responsible and levelheaded. If she is single, she is known as the maid of honor. If she is married, she is the matron of honor. She will calm the bride's jitters and help her make decisions.

The maid/matron of honor is involved in all aspects of wedding planning, including helping the bride select her gown and the attendants' attire. She is responsible for scheduling appointments for the bridesmaids' fittings and sometimes even their make-up and hair. She helps make calls to vendors, addresses invitations, makes reception favors or table decorations, and records wedding gifts received and thank you's sent.

The maid/matron of honor hosts a bridal shower for the bride and invites all of the bridesmaids. Other friends or members of the bride's family may be invited if this will be the only shower that the bride will have. The maid/matron of honor attends pre-wedding parties, the rehearsal, and the rehearsal dinner.

On the wedding day, the maid/matron of honor helps the bride get dressed, arranges the bride's veil and train before and during the ceremony, holds the bridal bouquet during the wedding service, and wears the groom's ring on her thumb until she gives it to the bride to put on the groom's finger. She prepares an emergency kit for the bride, consisting of needle, thread, extra nylons, tape, etc. She also carries a duplicate list of songs for the wedding singers or musicians, a duplicate list of readings or prayers and who reads what, and a duplicate list of selected shots for the photographer and videographer, The maid/matron of honor precedes the bride down the aisle. She also signs the marriage certificate, along with the groom, and bustles the bride's train before the reception.

After or before the ceremony, the maid/matron of honor joins in the formal photographs. She collects the bride's belongs from the changing room at the ceremony site and returns them later to the bride's home.

The maid/matron of honor stands next to the groom in the receiving line, sits next to him during the reception, and dances with him during the first dance. She carries another duplicate list of names and pronunciations for bridal party announcements and an extra song list for the DJ or the band. She also helps gather single women for the bouquet toss.

After the reception, she helps the bride change into her going away clothes. She takes the wedding gown to the dry cleaners for cleaning and preparation for storage or just brings it to the bride and groom's home. She may also take the bride's bouquet for preserving. In addition, she helps the best man collect the wedding gifts and takes them to the bride and groom's home.

The maid/matron of honor pays for her gown and accessories, her travel expenses, a shower gift for the bride, and a wedding gift for the bride and groom. She also may share the cost of the bridal shower with the other bridesmaids.

Duties of the Bridesmaids

The bridesmaids help the maid/matron of honor plan the wedding shower. They can sometimes help the bride with wedding plans. They walk behind the ushers during the processional or can be paired with them to go down the aisle as couples. They stand to the left of the maid/matron of honor in the receiving line and sit at the head table with the bride and groom, the best man, and the maid/matron of honor. e bridesmaids pay for their own gowns and accessories, their travel expenses, and a wedding gift for the bride and groom.

Some brides select junior bridesmaids because they have a lot of little sisters or cousins they want to include in their wedding. Junior bridesmaids usually are from eight to fourteen years old. Older sisters or cousins usually are regular bridesmaids. Junior bridesmaids usually don't help with wedding planning, though some older girls may be really helpful to the bride as go-fers and makers of wedding favors and table decorations. Sometimes these young ladies help make banners for the ceremony or fold wedding programs. For large weddings, brides will need all the help they can get and should put their responsible junior bridesmaids to work.

Junior bridesmaids (or rather their parents) pay for their gowns and accessories, their travel expenses, and a wedding gift for the bridal couple.

Duties of the Groomsmen/Ushers

The groomsmen or ushers help the best man with the bachelor party and help organize the transportation to the reception. They attend all pre-wedding parties, the rehearsal, and the rehearsal dinner.

The groomsmen's main job is to seat guests. They should arrive at the ceremony site at least an hour before the wedding service. They should know which side of the space to seat which guests. In Christian and many secular ceremonies, the bride's family is seated on the left and the groom's is on the right. In Jewish weddings, the bride's family is seated on the right and the groom's on the left. The ushers should offer each female guest their right arms, and her spouse or date should follow behind them. Ushers should lead male guests to their seats.

As they seat guests, the ushers pass out wedding programs. They show guests where to put their wedding gifts and ask them to sign a guest book if one is used.

Just before the wedding begins, the ushers should seat the groom's parents and then the bride's parents. This signals that the ceremony is about to start. The ushers then unroll the aisle runner, if one is used. If they are not part of the procession, the groomsmen will take their places at the front of the space, next to the groom and the best man.

After the ceremony, the groomsmen escort the bridesmaids from the ceremony space. They take part in formal photographs. One of the ushers should roll up the aisle runner and put it in a safe place. The ushers should pick up any leftover programs and give them to the bride and groom in case they want to send them to family and friends. The groomsmen dance with the bridesmaids during the first dance and help gather single men to participate in the garter toss.

The groomsmen pay for their own attire and transportation, wedding gifts for the couple, and contribute to valet parking at the reception.

Duties of the Flower Girl

A flower girl is not essential to every wedding. If there is a special child the bridal couple wants to honor or include in the wedding, she usually is chosen as the flower girl. Most flower girls are between three and seven years old. The flower girl goes down the aisle before the bride enters and sprinkles rose petals as she goes.

Duties of the Ringbearer

The ring bearer usually is a little boy the bride and groom want to include in the wedding. Like the flower girl, he is usually between three and seven years old. He often carries both rings, tied on a satin pillow. In some cases, the rings are put inside a box or other container. Often in medieval or fairy tale weddings, the rings are placed in little wooden boxes that are decorated like treasure chests.

Suggestions for a Stress-Free Ceremony

On the day of the wedding, everyone will be running on adrenalin. To keep everything running smoothly and to keep the bridal couple from booking a quiet, padded room at the local sanitarium, draft wedding checklists for each member of the wedding party. These could be made out soon after your wedding party has been selected so that everyone knows what to do.

Since the best man and the maid/matron of honor will act as stage managers and will be running the show, give them small booklets or small clipboards with their checklists. Tie a pen to the booklet or clipboard so they won't lose it. This way, they will remember to have an usher place the readings at the podium or other last minute details. They can also send someone to check on whether the musicians have everything they need and that the flowers have arrived and are in place.

Usually these duties fall to a professional wedding planner who is highly paid to run around like a maniac, making sure everything is done just so. Some wedding planners handle only the reception.

Before you engage one, make sure you know the scope of the wedding planner's responsibilities. In many weddings where the bridal couple is doing most of the work themselves, these duties have to land on someone. A member of the bridal party or the mother of the bride is the usual person who takes care of these details.

CHAPTER SIX

PUTTING ON THE RITZ: WEDDING ATTIRE

Choosing the Perfect Wedding Gown

For many women, choosing their wedding dress is one of the most exciting moments in their lives, as well as one of their biggest investments. Attire for the bride, groom, the bridesmaids, and the groomsmen usually comprises about 12 % of the wedding budget. For a $25,000 wedding, that breaks down to 11% or $2,500 for the bridal gown, veil, train, undergarments, jewelry, shoes, and any alterations for the bride and 1% or $250 for the groom's attire. (The bride usually allows another 1% of the budget for salon appointments to do her hair and makeup.)

Start looking for your dress at least nine months before the wedding. If you order the gown, allow four to six months for construction and shipping. Allow extra time for fittings. If you have your dress made or you order it, pad the deadline for when you need the gown. No matter how good the seamstress or the dress designer is, delays happen, so allow enough time to track your order or to reorder.

To choose the perfect dress, you will need to first consider the season of the year, whether the wedding will take place indoors or outdoors, and your wedding style. Since you will also need to choose your wedding colors before you shop for your attendants' dresses, you might want to keep those colors in mind when you look for your own dress. You may decide to choose a different fabric, weight, or shade or change the hue of your wedding colors. For example, you find the perfect ivory dress in shantung silk. Because this particular fabric has more weight and a deeper hue, it reflects light differently. You then decide to change your colors from lilac and pink to purple and rose.

If you are marrying in the summer, try to choose fabrics that breathe and are cooler in hot weather. If you are doing a tropical destination wedding, you want to make sure your gown is lightweight and is made from a natural fabrics. In any case, check the weather patterns for the particular location and time of year. You will need to match your perfect gown with the environment where the wedding will be held. All this detail will ensure that you and your bridal party are comfortable.

Always try on the gowns you pick out. They never look the same on the hanger as they will on a human body. And, be sure to try on several. Look at yourself in a three-way mirror. Observe how the material falls and how the light hits the dress. See how the waistline and bust line feel. Make sure you are comfortable everywhere in the dress. If you are not, ask the salesperson or dressmaker whether the dress can be altered. Notice any bunching or bulging. Check the embroidery, stitching, and beading to make sure that all are well sewn.

Take a good friend with you when you shop for your gown. Mothers and other friends often are so overcome just seeing you in a wedding gown that they will gush about how beautiful you are. But you are buying a dress that will be seen by a room full of guests (some of whom you may have never met before) and will be immortalized in photographs. You need someone who will be brutally honest and tell you whether that clingy jersey makes your butt look too big or that you really don't look good in stark white.

When the dress you have ordered arrives at the store, quickly make an appointment for a fitting. Don't wait until the last minute to do this. If there are problems with your dress, you will need time to have it fixed.

Some brides make the mistake of ordering their wedding dress a size or two smaller than their current size. This is wishful thinking. Unless you have had a gastric bypass and will be guaranteed to lose weight, ordering a smaller size is foolish and can be very costly. The stresses of planning a wedding can cause some brides to head for the chocolate. Order your current size. If you lose weight, it is always much easier to take in a dress than it is to let one out.

Deposits on wedding gowns are non-refundable and can be as much as half the cost of the dress. Be sure that you are very happy with your dress choice before you put any money down.

Gown Choices. For very formal weddings, a floor-length white or off-white dress is the traditional choice. Pair it with a cathedral or extended cathedral train and a full-length veil, long gloves or long sleeves. For a formal day or evening ceremony, choose a long gown with or without a short train and a fingertip veil or hat. Use a longer veil for evening and add gloves. A floor-length gown with a chapel veil is a good choice for a semi-formal wedding. You can also have a tea-length or ballerina-length dress with a fingertip veil. An informal wedding has the most choice for a wedding gown. It can be a street-length gown or a fancy lace suit with no veil, but a hat or floral hairpiece is appropriate. Theme wedding attire falls into this category.

Dress Style and Body Types. Finding the right dress style for your body type will help put you in a very flattering light. If you want to look taller, wear a high neckline or an off-the-shoulder gown or one with short sleeves or no sleeves.

If you are already statuesque, you can wear a drop waist with a wide belt or a low neckline with full sleeves. Ruffles that wrap around the body can also make you look shorter.

If you want to appear slender, a princess seemed A-line dress is very flattering, as well as a scoop or sweetheart neckline. Avoid puffy sleeves, ruffles, clingy fabrics such as crepe de chine or jersey, or bulky fabrics such as velvets or brocades. Strive for clean lines.

If you want to appear shapelier, choose heavier fabrics, ruffles, decorations around the bodice, and a gathered waist.

To de-emphasize specific areas of the body, here are some tricks. Wide hips can be disguised with a flared skirt and by drawing attention to bodice detail in lace or beading. Camouflaging a large bust is achieved by fitting the bodice and using a V-neck or high neck with a keyhole cutout. Avoid narrow waistlines and empire styles. If you are short waisted, A-line and drop waist bodices lengthen the silhouette. Petite women should avoid big, ball gowns; they will get lost in them.

Color. Before Queen Victoria, all brides, even as far back as biblical times, were married in blue, a color supposed to denote purity. Royal brides in England wore silver. Queen Victoria broke tradition and started one of her own by marrying in white. In keeping with this custom, for over a hundred years, only virgin brides wore white, and brides who had been married before or who had been living with a man wore off-white or cream dresses. That has passed by the wayside. Any bride can wear white or any color she wants. Some brides have chosen to wear a pastel or even a deep, rich color, especially if the wedding falls around a holiday or is a theme wedding.

Remarriages. Encore brides can even wear white but should avoid a long veil and a long trail. Having a little sweep to the gown or an off-the-face veil is considered appropriate, however. Hats and headpieces are great for encore brides. A traditional wedding gown is not always a good choice for an older bride. A cocktail dress, tea-length gown, and a dressy suit are also good choices.

Custom. For good luck, wealth, and prosperity in the marriage, many brides slip a penny in one of their shoes on their wedding day.

Bridesmaid's Dresses

In Medieval times, members of the bridal party dressed alike for two reasons. One ancient legend says that this would confuse evil spirits who wanted to harm the bride and groom. If the bridesmaids and the bride all wore the same thing and the groom and the groomsmen wore similar clothes, the evil spirits couldn't pick out the real bride and groom. Another story says that brides were often kidnapped by their prospective grooms. The bride's attendants, usually her ladies in waiting, dressed like the bride, so the groom and his men would be confused and kidnap the wrong woman. Whatever the case, the custom has continued that the members of the wedding party dress similarly.

Today, brides dress all of their attendants in one of the bridal colors. When you select gowns for your bridesmaids, make sure that you select styles that will be flattering for each body type. Choose fabrics that are comfortable for the season. A flower girl can wear a dress identical to the bridesmaids or she can have a white dress like the bride's or just a fancy long dress with a sash or bow that matches the color of the bridesmaid's dresses.

Not all of the dresses need to match exactly. You can dress your bridesmaids all in the same color but in different dress styles. You can put them in the same dress style but in different shades of your wedding colors or all in different colors.

Groom's and Groomsmen's Attire

Choices for the groom and the groomsmen are easier. For most weddings, the choice will be either a tuxedo or a suit. For a theme wedding or a destination wedding, the choices will naturally vary more and could be unusual. Like the bride's dress, the groom and his men will need to remember the season, the time of day, and the formality of the wedding when choosing clothing. Their attire should complement the bride's dress and her choice of wedding colors.

For a very formal evening wedding, the groom should wear black tails with a white, wing-collar shirt, white bow tie, and pleated solid black or black striped trousers. Add patent leather shoes, a top hat, and cane, and the very formal look is complete. The bride's wedding colors can be shown in the color of the boutonnieres.

A very formal daytime wedding usually requires the groom to wear a dark gray cutaway coat with gray striped trousers. He wears a white, wing-collar shirt and an ascot, and may also complete his formal look with a top hat, spats, and gray gloves.

A black tuxedo with a white tuxedo shirt is appropriate for a formal evening wedding. The groom wears a black bow tie and a cummerbund or vest. For a formal daytime wedding, the groom wears a gray waistcoat or cutaway or even a black or gray stroller jacket, with striped trousers, a white wing-collar shirt, and striped tie.

A semi-formal evening wedding calls for a black tuxedo or dinner jacket, a white shirt, black bow tie, and a vest or cummerbund in one of the bride's wedding colors. A white dinner jacket can be worn during the summer months or for a tropical destination wedding. A dark suit is also acceptable.

For a semi-formal daytime wedding, the groom wears a gray stroller coat, pinstripe trousers, a turned-down collar shirt, tie, and a vest. A dark, formal suit with dark trousers and a white shirt is also appropriate. Again a cummerbund or vest and a tie or bow tie with dark shoes and black socks completes the groom's attire. In summer, a lighter colored formal suit can be worn.

Informal daytime and evening weddings require only a business suit and tie. For an outdoor beach wedding or a theme wedding, the groom can wear a white, gauzy cotton shirt or even a tropical or Hawaiian shirt. Embroidered wedding shirts are still popular for informal outdoor weddings.

The groomsmen should wear something slightly different from the groom so that he stands out. Sometimes, this is just a slight change in the color of the bow ties they wear. At other times, groomsmen select a different style or color of their tuxedoes or suits. The bride's wedding colors are often shown in the color choices of the bow ties, the cummerbunds, or even the dress shirts the men wear.

If you choose a period wedding or other type of theme wedding, the wedding clothes for the groom and groomsmen will need to reflect the era chosen, the cultural group, or the bit of fantasy the wedding couple wants. This often results in contacting a costumer or skilled seamstress or tailor to make the clothing for the event. If you plan to make much of the clothing yourself, there are period clothing and costume patterns available from the popular pattern companies. You can also search the Internet for suitable patterns or vendors who can make your wedding garments for you. However, make sure you order your wedding clothing well in advance so that alterations can be made if necessary.

Measuring for Men's Formal Clothing

It is important to measure correctly when ordering formal attire. This is crucial if you are flying to another city and will pick up your formal wear there. The easiest way to do this is to go to a formal wear shop and have the salesperson measure you. Ask him or her to write down your sizes so that you can send them to the formal wear store in the other city. Before you do that, try on a few jackets and trousers from the formal wear shop in your town to make sure that all of the sizes are correct.

Of particular importance is making sure that the salesperson is measuring you correctly. Chest and waist sizes are usually easy to do. Some salespeople ask that you take a breath when they measure your chest. This usually isn't necessary because there should be enough ease in the clothing so that you can breath easily and cross your arms in front of you. The inseam is also easy to do. Measure from your crotch to the desired length on the inside of your leg. Ask the salesperson what is the current pants length if you are uncertain what your length should be for formal wear.

Measuring the shirt size is where some sales people trip up. The neck size is simply the circumference of your neck. This determines the shirt size. A 16-inch neck is a size 16 shirt. Measure the sleeve length from the neck vertebrae to the wrist bone. Make sure that you bend your elbow. Take the next size up if the measurement falls between sizes. For example, if you measure 33 ½ inches, take a size 34 sleeve. If you have long arms, try not to let the salesperson talk you into getting a bigger size shirt to accommodate your sleeve length. For example, if you wear a size 35 sleeve or longer but have a size 16 neck or less, don't go up to a size 17 or larger shirt. Unless the shop offers alterations, don't go in that direction. Insist on a size 16 shirt with a 35 sleeve. Reputable formal wear shops can usually get any size configuration you need.

Check with the salesperson about how much shirtsleeve is supposed to show under the suit or tuxedo. This, like pants length, does vary with fashion.

Today, there are also widely different suit and tuxedo fits. There are fuller cut jackets with lots of ease in them. There are athletic cuts that accommodate broad shoulders and can even cover a bigger belly, if the man's shoulders are big. There are Italian cut suits that have a short rise and fit very snuggly over the behind.

Other Clothing Choices

The ring bearer can either wear something identical to the groom or he can match the groomsmen. If the ring bearer is the groom's own son, he might choose to have him look just like Daddy. If there is also a flower girl in the wedding party, the ring bearer's clothing could complement hers by having his bowtie or vest match her dress color.

The bride's and groom's fathers can wear tuxedoes, but the style doesn't have to match the groom's or the groomsmen's attire. The fathers will usually choose something that complements their wives' formal gowns.

The mothers of the bridal couple can either wear dresses in a slightly different shade of the bridesmaids' dresses. The style and cut can be very different, though the length is usually the same. If the bridesmaids are wearing floor length gowns, the mothers usually do, too. Sometimes, the mothers just wear whatever color flatters them the most.

Accessories

Don't forget ties, cummerbunds, shoes, spats, socks, underwear, and possibly gloves and hats for the men. All of the women in the wedding party will need jewelry, shoes, undergarments, and nylons. They may also need hats and gloves. In some cases, they may need parasols, fans, or tiny purses, depending on your wedding style and theme.

Women's wedding shoes are usually dyed the same color as their gowns. The bride's shoes often are white or crème satin. If she is wearing a colored suit or dress, then the shoes are usually the same color or are white.

If the wedding is a beach ceremony or one outdoors on a carpet of grass, the bride may also chose to go barefoot. That doesn't mean that the bride doesn't wear anything on her feet. She can chose to wear an ankle bracelet or handmade foot jewelry that wraps around the ankle and loops over the second toe. These are similar to the Middle Eastern bracelets that also have a ring attached to a chain on the bracelet.

CHAPTER SEVEN

CHERISHED TREASURES: WEDDING RINGS AND GIFTS

History of the Engagement Ring and the Wedding Ring

Pope Innocent III was responsible for the custom of two rings: the engagement ring and the wedding ring. He insisted on a waiting period between the engagement and the marriage. Since each was a contract, a ring was given to seal the legal deal. Prior to the 13th century, only the engagement ring was given in Europe, though the wedding ring was far older.

Almost five thousand years ago, Egyptians exchanged reed or hemp rings as symbols of eternity, a circle with no end. During biblical times, great dowry gifts were given at a couple's betrothal. It has been speculated that a ring, especially one of precious metal, was substituted as a less expensive dowry.

The Romans used rings as seals and to denote ownership, with high-ranking senators wearing gold ones and ordinary citizens using iron ones. These were related to the large iron rings that held the keys to the household. It has been speculated that when a Roman citizen gave his bride an iron wedding ring, he was actually giving her the keys to his household and all his worldly goods.

In 16th century England, the marriage ring was officially moved from the right hand to the left. Some think this change was to show a woman her place, since the right hand was considered the hand of power. The placement of the ring on the third finger was supposed to be the place where the *vena amoris* or love vein connected that finger directly to the heart.

The Puritans thought rings were heathen so did not use them in their wedding ceremonies. They did, however, exchanged wedding thimbles because they were practical. The Victorians embraced the custom of the wedding ring wholeheartedly and embellished their rings with twin hearts and flowers. The Edwardians added delicate filigree and leaf patterns. Art deco rings became streamlined, modern, and abstract.

Men generally never wore wedding rings until WW II. Soldiers going off to war decided to wear wedding rings in order to remember their wives back home. Today, most marriages are double ring ceremonies, meaning that both the bride and groom are given rings to show their commitment and love.

Choosing a Wedding Band

Most jewelers will tell you that the general rule for buying an engagement ring is buy one that costs as much as two to three months' salary. That's thousands of dollars. Not only will the young groom have to save for a long time in order to buy such a ring, but he will also have to make a judgment call about the size of the ring because most engagement rings are bought without the woman's knowledge. Though this is romantic, it really leaves the choice of ring to the groom and the jeweler he uses. There also is the problem of matching the engagement ring with the wedding band.

Some couples keep the excitement and romance of the man "popping the question" unexpectedly by giving something else as a token or just asking the woman to marry him in a romantic way. The selection of an engagement ring is then done together as they would pick out their wedding rings later.

One young man we know gave his intended bride a water-smoothed stone from his favorite spot on a lakeshore where he grew up. The bride made a wire setting for it and wore it as a necklace. It had special meaning when the bride wore it on their wedding day as they were married on the shore of that same lake.

Though buying a diamond engagement ring can cost as much as a down payment on a house and may take as long to pay off as a mortgage, wedding rings need not be that expensive. Usually, they are a few hundred dollars for both rings, and can be as little as a hundred. Another couple we know had an artist dye cast their rings from melted down estate silverware. Those rings were unique and only cost $10 dollars apiece thirty years ago. Even when the bride had to have her ring resized, it was easily stretched and kept the original design true.

Metals. In the 21st century, wedding rings are not just gold or silver, they can be almost any metal, either plain or with gem settings. Some new wedding bands are thin rings of ruby or sapphire, and some even have fine bits of metal inlaid into the band. In addition, some bridal couples are looking at buying estate jewelry and having it reset

The choice of metal is really personal though the properties of each metal should be taken into consideration. Gold is traditional, but it can abrade because it is a soft metal. Likewise, silver is soft but stronger than gold and seems to be more easily malleable for intricate designs.

Platinum is a modern choice but is more durable than gold, though it can scratch. It also is more expensive than gold. Because platinum is coated in rhodium (and so is white gold), you may need to have your ring re-plated after two or three years.

If you choose to have a two-toned ring, use platinum and yellow gold or white gold and some other metal such as copper or brass. These other metals are often used in inlaid work.

Titanium is the ring choice of the 21st century. It is highly durable, doesn't need polishing, and looks sleek and modern. Because it is a harder metal, rings in titanium cannot be re-sized.

Furthermore, make note of the styles of wedding bands. They come in half round (round on the outside, flat on the inside), comfort fit or court shape (round inside and outside), flat (flat on both sides), and flat comfort fit or flat court shape (flat on the outside and round on the inside). These different styles offer a range of comfort. Try on several styles to determine what is most comfortable on your particular hand.

Whatever wedding rings you choose, try on several different metals, designs, and band widths. Seeing how each ring looks on your hand will help you make a decision that you will be happy with for a lifetime.

Gifts for Wedding Participants

The bridal couple often gives gifts to the members of the wedding party. The best man and maid/matron of honor usually get a bigger or more special gift. Sometimes, it is some part of the wedding attire that the bride gives to her attendants, such as jewelry. It can also be a spa day where the bride and her bridesmaids get facials and massages as the bride's gift. The nature of the gift can be anything from handmade remembrance books to tickets to a concert or even CDs. Often, in a theme wedding, the bride gives something that is tied to the theme. For example, in a fairy wedding where the attendants and the bride wear fairy wings, the bridesmaids may be given the wings as gifts.

The gifts for the best man and the groomsmen can be almost anything. Some grooms have given money clips and tie tacks. Some best men have even received watches as gifts. Again, tickets to sporting events or concerts are good choices, as well as CDs and books. Sometimes, a simple gift certificate to a favorite restaurant or club is a good choice.

These gifts are an expression of your appreciation for the people who stood up with you in your wedding. They should reflect how well you know these people and should be something that they will enjoy. Moreover, these gifts don't have to be expensive. They can be homemade or store bought, classic or unique.

To Register or Not

Because couples today are marrying later, they have lived on their own for some time. They will have some household items, including dishes and small appliances. That is why it is very important for couples to list what they need at gift registries. You don't have to just note your preferences for fine china and flatware; you can choose tools and other home improvement items, camping gear, and even vacations. There are online registries as well as brick-and-mortar ones.

Set up your registry early so that guests can make their choices for you as they learn about your wedding. Generally, couples register eight to nine months before the wedding day, and some do it up to a year and a half in advance. Don't have your registry engraved on your wedding invitation, but allow your family and wedding party to notify guests when they ask. Also, remember to select items in all price ranges. Some friends and family members may feel comfortable combining funds and selecting a more expensive gif,t but don't expect everyone to do that if they can't afford to buy the pricey items you've chosen. In addition, registering online at a store that is found in many cities throughout the country gives your guests the convenience of selecting gifts in their hometowns and taking them to the wedding. They can also choose to have the gifts sent to the bride's home.

Wedding Gifts for Encore Couples

Today, it is proper for encore couples to register for gifts just as they did for their first marriages. This is especially important because many encore couples already have enough pots and pans and other household items. By consulting a wedding registry, guests may choose items that the couple really needs. Some encore couples select sports equipment, barbeque gear, or gifts to use on their honeymoon. Some couples forgo gifts altogether and invite guests to make a donation to the couple's favorite charity.

CHAPTER EIGHT

PRINTED DETAILS: INVITATIONS, PROGRAMS, AND ANNOUNCEMENTS

Invitations

Deciding on your wedding guest list can be a royal battle when you are dealing with two families, each with its own lists of can't-forget relatives and must-invite friends. This is the couple's first major test of the ability to compromise. There are no rules or guidelines about wedding guest lists. Budget is the only limiting factor.

The average stationery budget comprises about 4% of the entire wedding budget. For a $25,000 wedding, that comes to $1,000. This budget figure includes the price of the invitations, envelopes, wedding programs, cards for the tables at the reception, and thank you cards. Printed (commonly called engraved) invitations cost anywhere from $100 to $500 per 100. When you add on printed return addresses and inserts, such as reception RSVP cards and their envelopes, the price increases. Some companies also charge extra for envelopes—and there are two: an inner envelope that contains the personal salutation and an outer one that has all of the postal information on it.

Importantly, couples should remember that each guest they invite will add to their total wedding costs. A large guest list will not make your wedding better, nor will it make your marriage last longer. By inviting only people you really care about will make this beautiful day extra special and keep the crowd of well-wishers manageable.

Styles. Wedding invitations should reflect your wedding style. If you are planning a formal or semi-formal wedding, most wedding invitations offered by stationery or wedding printing companies will fit the bill. All you will need to do is find the particular kind of invitation you like that you can afford. Most of the formal styles have black ink on white or crème colored paper, with matching envelopes. Sometimes silver or pale pink embellishments are added, but there is usually very little color.

Though these invitations will always please Emily Post, technology has opened a creative door for many bridal couples. Some wedding stationery companies are offering color photographs and reproductions of paintings on the invitation cover, with poetry or scripture verses. These invitations are quite attractive and capture the romance of the occasion. They are becoming very popular for semi-formal and informal weddings.

With today's computers, couples can also create their own invitations. Home printers can produce a professional look, especial when printed on premium paper. Though tech savvy and creative couples can produce unique invitations, there are software programs available that are formatted for the correct card size. These have several options that may be dropped into the invitation template. Some couples have just used a plain card template and imported photos, drawings, or wedding clip art to create invitations. Special fonts, especially those that look like calligraphy, add an elegant touch.

Another personal touch for the crafter is the handmade invitation using rubber stamps, paints, and inks. Scrapbookers can apply their skills to invitations, as well as watercolorists and other visual artists. These invitations become lasting keepsakes for those who are invited.

Some brides have used colored sealing wax and an engraved seal to close the envelopes for their invitations. This adds romance, especially if you choose a Victorian or a Valentine's Day theme.

For encore couples, tradition has dictated that the bride hand-write the invitation or make phone calls. Since there are more and more remarriages happening today, formal engraved invitations save the bride's valuable time and have become socially acceptable.

Anatomy of an Invitation. The purpose of a wedding invitation is to invite someone to attend your wedding. The hosting couple, usually the parents, invites the guests.

Mr. and Mrs. Harold West
Request the honor of your presence
At the marriage of their daughter
Elizabeth West
To
Mr. Stephen North
Saturday, the eighteenth of June
Two Thousand Five
At Holy Cross Church
Sixteen Main Street
Your Town, New York

If the couple is paying for the wedding themselves and acting as hosts, the invitation is worded differently.

Miss Elizabeth West and Mr. Stephen North
Request the honor of your presence
At their marriage
Saturday, the eighteenth of June
Two Thousand Five
At Holy Cross Church
Sixteen Main Street
Your Town, New York

There are variations that you can use in your invitations. You can say that you and your groom invite the guest "to share our joy at our marriage" or "request the honor of your presence as we join in holy matrimony" or "request the honor of your presence as we exchange our vows" or "invite you to witness as we exchange marriage vows" or "request the pleasure of your company at our wedding" or even "invite you to join us as we exchange marriage vows." Use your imagination to create just the right tone.

If you are remarrying, the invitation comes from the bridal couple or their children.

Susan and Thomas Johnson
and
Alice and Brian Anderson
Request the honor of your presence
At the marriage of their parents
Rachel Johnson
and
Bruce Anderson
Saturday, the eighteenth of June
Two Thousand Five
At Holy Cross Church
Sixteen Main Street
Your Town, New York

Some couples see a remarriage as the joining of two families. Their wedding invitations can reflect that.

Rachel Johnson
With her daughter Susan and her son
Thomas Johnson
and
Bruce Anderson
With his daughter Alice and his son Brian Anderson
Request the honor of your presence
At their marriage
Saturday, the eighteenth of June
Two Thousand Five
At Holy Cross Church
Sixteen Main Street
Your Town, New York

Etiquette mavens state that couples should not include their gift registry information on the invitation because it looks as if they are begging for gifts. They also say not to put a "No Gifts, please" note on the invitation nor to indicate a charity to give a donation to in lieu of a gift. The decision to offer a gift to the bridal couple is always optional, the etiquette gurus say. It is a reaction to the joy of hearing about someone's marriage. Therefore, such restrictions would be correct information for a very formal invitation.

In practice, it has become a requirement to bring a gift when attending a wedding. In addition, in this era where friends and family are spread all over the globe, it may be easier to indicate gift information on a separate card and enclose it with the RSVP card. This actually becomes a courtesy for out-of-town friends and family. Otherwise, each guest would have to call the bride, the groom, or their parents to find out this information. Frankly, just getting guests to return RSVP catering cards is difficult enough. In addition, some of those invited may just be business acquaintances or friends of the family who might feel awkward calling the couples' families for gift information.

When to Order. Place your order for invitations well in advance, usually about six to nine months before your wedding. Always order a few more invitations than you think you'll need or ask for five to ten extra envelopes. That's a good backup plan since it's easy to make mistakes when addressing envelopes.

You should receive your invitations in a couple of months. Start addressing them about two to four months before the wedding. This monumental task can be done in several sessions using the help of your bridal party and your parents. Use an organized list that you've printed out from your computer. This way, you can give portions of the list to different people without losing any vital information. If you keep a master list on your computer, you can quickly check off guests, by inserting a check mark on one side of the name for "Sent" and a check mark or number on the other side to indicate the person is coming or the total number of people coming from each household. This will simplify your head-counts for your caterer. As your responses come in, you can also indicate who might need help with accommodations or transportation.

Addressing. Most invitations have an outer envelope for all of the postal information and an inner envelope to include a personal note. For the most part, invitations will be easy to address. Simple Mr. and Mrs. will do for most people, and Miss, Mr., and Ms. usually covers the rest. There are a couple of instances that you should be aware of. For a couple living together but not married, on the outer envelope put the woman's full first name on one line and the man's below hers. If a woman has kept her maiden name, both names are written on the same line. In the case of two doctors who are married, the invitation can be addressed as "The Doctors Smith" or "Dr. Julia Smith and Dr. James Smith."
The inner envelope adds warmth to even formal invitations. Though the outer one says "Mr. and Mrs. Theodore Mason," you can address the inner envelope, "Uncle T and Aunt Julie," if that is how you refer to them. The inner envelope is the place to add children of the couple you are inviting. For example, the outer envelope will say "Sarah Jones and Bill Williams" but the inner envelope will say "Sarah and Bill and Suzie and Brian." For a more formal invitation, the inner envelope will say "Ms. Jones, Mr. Williams, Suzie and Brian." Lists of names like this can be written all in one line or in a vertical column.

Ms. Jones
Mr. William
Suzie and Brian

Stuffing Envelopes. To simplify and speed up the stuffing process, set up an assembly line with two or three people. Arrange stacks, printing side up, of enclosure cards, enclosure envelopes, invitations, addressed inner envelopes, addressed outer envelopes, and stamps. Put an enclosure card on top of its envelope, making sure the point of the envelope flap falls over the printed face of the card. Put the enclosure on top of the invitation. Turn everything over and place in the inner envelope. Check the name on the envelope and match it to the outer envelope. Seal and put on a stamp.

After sealing, you can stop and do the stamping at another session. Before you take your invitations to the post office, group the envelopes by zip code. The post office prefers this step when sending out mass mailings. It makes their lives easier and will help make sure your precious invitations get where they are going. For those sent out of the country, leave the envelope unsealed. Often international letters are inspected. If you are unsure about this, call your local post office and ask what their policy is regarding international mail.

Ceremony Programs

For nearly all wedding ceremonies, you will need some way to identify participants in the wedding. Usually, this takes the form of a wedding program. These are similar to the programs that are passed out in church or at school functions. They tell the order of the service, who reads what and when, and who the singers and musicians are. They also identify who is in the wedding party, who the celebrant is, who the parents are, and nearly everyone who helped with the wedding. They are extremely helpful if you are having a cultural or religious wedding and some of your guests are unfamiliar with the rituals and customs you will be using.

Wedding programs can be professionally printed in the same style as your invitations. They can also be printed on home computers just as a church bulletin or a school concert flyer. Both are perfectly acceptable. Wedding programs can be just a single sheet of decorative paper or a small wedding booklet. Whatever the size or style, your wedding program will become a treasured souvenir of your wedding day.

Ideally, the wedding program should be printed as close to the wedding day as possible. That ensures that any changes in the location of your ceremony or reception or in the people involved in your wedding will be reflected in the wedding program. Negotiate with your printer early on to guarantee a timely delivery. Draft a rough copy a few weeks before the wedding to make sure everyone's name is spelled correctly and to record any last minute changes in music or readings. Make a corrected copy and take it to your printer or run off copies from your computer. If you do it yourself, allow time to assemble or fold the programs.

Inside the Wedding Program. What you decide to put on your wedding program really depends on the nature of your wedding service. You can just list the order of the service and the list of participant, or you can create a complete booklet with a cover and special acknowledgements.

Cover. This acts as a title page and bears the names of the bride and groom and the date of the wedding. It can also include the time and place of the ceremony. Sometimes, the cover has a photo or artwork.

Order of Events. This lists the order of the events and the songs and readings. If you haven't included the time and place of the wedding on the cover, put it at the top of this page. Below this, outline what will happen, beginning with either the pre-music or the processional music. The order of the ceremony will depend on whether it is a civil or religious service, and even what type of religious ceremony. Generally, it includes a greeting by the celebrant, readings, prayers, a song or two, the exchange of vows, the rings, pronouncement of marriage, and the recessional music. There may be additions to this list such as the unity candle or the presentation of the elements (usually in a Catholic service where the wine is brought forward during the processional).

List of Participants. Group the participants according to their importance. List the names and relationship to the bridal couple. They are listed in the following order: the celebrant, the parents of the bride, the parents of the groom, grandparents, the best man and maid/matron of honor, the bridesmaids and groomsmen, the flower girl and ring bearer, the soloists, the musicians, the readers, the person in charge of the wedding book, the cake server, and anyone else who has a part in the ceremony or the reception. If flowers or banners were handmade by someone special, not a vendor, you can include those people's names as well. In addition, if the photographer or videographer was a friend, include the person's name as well.

Special Thanks. This is optional, but it is a place where you might recognize someone, not of the wedding party, who was very helpful in putting your wedding together. Again, this should not be a professional vendor.

Notes. Here you can briefly explain certain practices that are not explained by the celebrant. For example, if you are having an African or Celtic wedding and the bridal couple will be jumping over a broom, you may want to explain the basis for the custom.

Directions to the Reception. Some wedding programs insert a small sheet with directions to where the reception will be held if it is not in the same facility as the wedding. If it is in the same building, a small note is included at the end of the program, such as "A reception follows immediately in the church hall."

Options. If you want your guests to participate in a portion of the ceremony, such as singing, communion, or in the affirmation of the marriage in some way, invite them with a small note. You can also place asterisks in areas where you want extra participation. Also, if there are special responses you want the congregation to do, indicate them.

At the end of the wedding program, you can also mention memorials. For example, "On this day of happiness, we would like to remember those who are no longer with us, especially Rose Smith, the bride's grandmother, and George Thompson, the groom's late uncle." You can also indicate that a special memorial candle was lit at the start of the service for someone who has passed away. (Lighting such a candle will depend on the church rules where your ceremony is held.)
Finally, you can include an explanation of the importance of the ceremony or reception location, the theme, or the song for the first dance. For example, if the bridal couple met in a garden behind the campus art museum and that is where the ceremony is held, you might note, "Smith Gardens is the place where John and Mary first met." Information like this deepens the experience for everyone invited.
You can also include a poem, quotation, or scripture on your wedding program.

Wedding Announcements and At Home Cards

Many couples send out wedding announcement to people they didn't invite to the wedding. Sometimes, they are even sent to people they invited because wedding announcements also include the new address and phone numbers for the couple. Sometimes, a small wedding snapshot is enclosed.

The wedding announcement just tells when the marriage occurred.

Linda Smith and Robert Jones
were married
Saturday, the eighteenth of May
Two Thousand Five
Holy Rock Church
Sixteen Main Street
Your Town, New York

Mr. and Mrs. John Smith
announce the marriage of their daughter
Linda
to
Mr. Robert Jones
Saturday, the eighteenth of May
Two Thousand Five
Holy Rock Church
Sixteen Main Street
Your Town, New York

If you will be away for a long honeymoon, you can send out At Home Cards. These state when you will be back in your new home and include your new address and phone number.

At home
after the first of July
Linda Smith and Robert Jones
42 Anyplace Ct., apt. 3
Your Town, New York 00001

At home
after the first of July
Mr. and Mrs. Robert Jones
42 Anyplace Ct., apt. 3
Your Town, New York 00001

Thank You Cards

Bridal couples can order thank you cards that match their invitations. They can also print out thank you cards using a small card template on their computers, especially if they want them to look like their custom-made computer invitations. They may also purchase thank you cards at any stationery store.

Couples should send out their last thank you's no later than a month after the wedding. Many gifts are sent in the mail or delivered some time before the wedding, though most wedding guests still bring their gifts along to the ceremony. To streamline this process and yet give each giver a proper thank you, the bridal couple can write out thank you notes as gifts arrive. You will be compiling a list of who sent what gift anyway. By taking a few moments to sit with the gift and the accompanying card, the couple can fully appreciate the gift and be able to express their gratitude to the person who sent it.

For the bulk of the gifts that are dropped off at the wedding, take a few days when you return from your honeymoon and unpack your gifts. Write a few thank you notes each day as you find special places for your gifts.

CHAPTER NINE

DELIGHTS OF THE SENSES: WEDDING FLOWERS

Flower Lore

Flowers at weddings have ancient roots. For centuries, strong scented herbs, spices, and flowers were placed in houses, at sacred sites, and were worn or carried. They were believed to ward off evil, bad luck, and even illness. Hence, the old legends about garlic protecting against evil. During the Roman Empire, wedding couples wore flower garlands as a symbol of new beginnings and fertility. The bridal bouquet itself signified a woman in full bloom. During the Victorian era, flowers took on heightened romance. Men and women gave each other flowers, with each kind of plant representing a secret message. Many brides today still use some of this symbolism in the bride's bouquet.

Flower Meanings

Some flowers have dual meanings. Lilies, for example, are often associated with funerals, but they are used in weddings to symbolize purity. Some brides avoid peonies because they are said to represent shame. However, peonies, to others, denote a happy marriage.

Though people from different cultures attach different meanings to the same flowers, there are some general attributes for each.

Flower Attributes	
Apple Blossoms – You are my perfect choice	Iris – Faith and hope
Baby's Breath – Pure of heart	Lilac – Youthfulness
Bachelor's Button – Blessedness	Orange Blossoms – Purity
Bells of Ireland – Good luck	Orchid – Love, beauty
Carnation – Pure and deep love	Rose, red – Love
Cattails – Peace and prosperity	Rose, pink – Happiness
Chrysanthemum – Abundance	Rose, white – Innocence
Daffodil – Respect	Rose, yellow – Tempered love
Daisy – Loyalty, innocence	Sunflowers- Pride
Gardenia – Loveliness	Tiger Lily – Pride and prosperity

Budget

As you begin to think about the flowers for your wedding, keep in mind that the cost of flowers comprises about 7% of your budget. For a $25,000 wedding, that comes to $1,750 for all of the flowers for the ceremony and reception. You can adjust this figure, up or down, depending on the flowers that you choose. Start looking for a florist as soon as possible. Select one between six and nine months before your wedding day.

How Many?

One of the first decisions you will need to make is defining how many places you will need flowers and how many floral types you will need. A very basic, small wedding can get by with the bride's bouquet and a boutonniere for the groom. An upscale wedding can call for two bridal bouquets (one to carry and one to toss), flowers for all the bridesmaids, boutonnieres for the groom and his groomsmen, corsages for the couple's mothers and grandmothers, boutonnieres for the fathers and grandfathers, a flower basket for the flower girl, boutonnieres for the ushers and the ring bearer, and possibly flowers for special aunts and uncles. Then there are flowers for the church (up to several arrangements), clusters of flowers at the end of each pew, flowers for the reception site, centerpieces for all the tables, and even flowers adorning the limousine. Some of these elaborate weddings also include flowers for the rehearsal dinner, flowers for out-of-town guests, and even floral hair ornaments for the bride and bridesmaids. Most weddings are somewhere in between these two extremes.

Styles change from time to time. Currently, styles of bridal bouquets are tight, French domes, ala Martha Stewart, with one type and color of flower. Long cascading bouquets, though used less at the moment, are still popular and would be so in Victorian or richly, romantic weddings. Reception table centerpieces today are simple 8" goldfish bowls of mixed garden flowers and greens. Most florists and wedding planners are reporting that modern brides are looking for something that reflects their individuality rather than convention. They also want more powerful colors in their flowers and, sometimes, unusual varieties.

Live or Silk?

The choice between live flowers or silk ones is really a matter of personal preference. Silk flowers aren't necessarily less expensive than live flowers. Nor is one choice more chic than another.

Some dressmakers and silk floral designers can create exquisite bridal bouquets and centerpieces. You don't need to worry about them wilting on your wedding day nor getting crushed in transport. Your silk bridal bouquet can easily be preserved under glass, in a container, or transformed into wall art.

You can even combine live and silk arrangements. For example, your altar flowers might be live flowers and left as a donation to the church while your bouquet and all the other flowers are silk. And some floral designers often create silk arrangements but incorporate some live flowers or greenery into their designs.

Nevertheless, some brides just prefer the aesthetics of live flowers. You will need to decide whether or not you want the scent of flowers at your wedding or prefer the durability of silk.

Homemade or Professional?

The next choice you will need to make is deciding whether you will use a florist or other professional floral designer or whether you will have a friend or family member make your floral arrangements. Some brides or one of the bridesmaid's often choose to do the flowers themselves. We know of one mother of the bride who spent her entire summer collecting wild grasses, seed heads, wheat, cattails, and oak leaves for her daughter's fall wedding. She combined these dried elements with fresh sunflowers bought from a florist.

Choosing a Florist

After you determine what your floral budget is and you have chosen your bridal colors, start talking with friends and family about floral designers. This kind of word of mouth will tell you more than any website or salesperson ever will. You can also ask for recommendations from sources at the ceremony site and the reception site.

Visit some of the florists that are suggested to you. See how they treat you as a potential customer, looking at their wares, but without mentioning that you are planning a wedding. Examine the flowers for freshness and note the shop's range of floral materials. Look over their displays. If they work with silk flowers, there is often a book of examples to show what kinds of arrangements they can make. If you can get a glimpse of the workroom, look at their stock of materials and see if the work area is well organized. Though a creative person can be messy, you want to make sure that your wedding flowers will not become soiled or lost underneath clutter. If you find a particular florist you'd like to try, have your finance order flowers for you or order them for yourself. See how you are treated, what the flower arrangement looks like when it is delivered, and whether the item was delivered in a timely manner.

When you have narrowed your choice to three floral arrangers, make an appointment for you and your groom to discuss flowers for your wedding. Draft a preliminary list of flowers that includes the number of bouquets, boutonnieres, corsages, and arrangements that you think you will need. Bring this list, along with pictures or swatches of your dress and the bridesmaids' dresses. Clip pictures from magazines of bouquets and flower arrangements that you like and take them to the meeting with the florist.

As you discuss your needs, ask to see photos of the florist's work. Find out if the florist has used the venues you have selected for your ceremony and reception. If your ceremony site is unusual (for example, in a state park or public garden), ask about the florist's experience with that kind of site. Seek suggestions from the florist. A professional with a creative eye will be able to suggest floral materials, ribbon colors, and other items that will fit right your requests. Ask about seasonal flowers since these often cost less. In addition, find out if the florist is able to do floral preservation for your bridal bouquet after the wedding.

Take detailed notes and ask for an estimate in writing. Also, ask about what is included in your final costs. Does the estimate include delivery, setup, and transportation fees? This is especially important if you are ordering exotic flowers. At this point, ask about refunds and what happens if something goes wrong on the day of the wedding.

Go home and look over the three estimates that you have. Once you decide on the one that will be best for you, make another appointment with the florist you've chosen. Discuss your final choices with the florist and have a formal contract drawn up. Make sure that you include as much information as possible, including the number of arrangements, what flowers are to be in each one, where the flowers will be delivered, when they will be delivered, and the amount all of this will cost. Also, ask if the florist will come with you to the ceremony and reception sites to discuss placement of the floral arrangements.

When you have all the details in place, sign the contract. You may need to put down a deposit. If you do, get a written receipt.

At least a month before the wedding, call the florist and confirm the wedding date and location. Remind the florist of everything that you have agreed upon. Check again a week or two before the wedding to make sure that everything is in place. Though you may be extra stressed at this time, double checking all vendors is always a good idea.

Bride's Bouquet

The bride's flowers set the tone for the rest of the floral pieces in the wedding. She can carry a lavish bouquet or a single rose. She may also carry a small prayer book or bible or other religious article that is decorated with flowers, instead of a bouquet.

Some brides request that the florist arrange two loose flowers within her bouquet. As the bride proceeds down the aisle, she can pull out one loose flower and hand it to her mother. After the ceremony, as she and the groom go up the aisle, she can stop and pull out the other loose flower and give it to her new mother-in-law. The bride can use this same idea to honor a grandmother or other important woman in her life.

Bridal Bouquet Styles

Arm Bouquet: Meant to be held in the crook of one arm, this large bouquet has a larger concentration of flowers near the crook of the arm that holds the flowers.

Biedermeier Bouquet: Concentric clusters of flowers.

Cascade: A large trailing arrangement, beginning from a round ball of flowers that cascades to the floor.

Hand-tied Bouquet: A cluster of long stem flowers tied with a ribbon. It may also be held in the crook of the arm if it is big enough.

Nosegay: A round, tight cluster of flowers.

Pomander: A ball of flowers tied to the wrist with decorative ribbons.

Spray Bouquet: A triangular cluster of flowers, with the base bigger than the top.

Single Flower: Can be any type of flower, from a rose to an orchid.

Flowers for the Bridal Party

Bridesmaids' Flowers. Flowers for the attendants are usually smaller versions of the bride's bouquet. They are often done in different colors. Some brides are opting to have their attendants carry flowers that are completely different from their own or the same flowers but in different colors. Bridesmaids can also carry baskets of flowers. Sometimes, if the bride is carrying a single flower, the attendant's can also carry single flowers as well or they can carry a full bouquet.

The maid/matron of honor may carry identical flowers as the other attendants, but she usually wears a different color dress. When she wears similar clothes as the other bridesmaids, she usually carries a different bouquet.

Groom and Groomsmen. Boutonnieres are the usual fare for the groom and groomsmen. They are identical, though the groom's can have an extra flower or has a different color flower or ribbons. There usually is something that distinguishes his boutonniere from the others.

Ring Bearers and Flower Girls. Very young children will play with a corsage or boutonniere. You also need to be very careful about pinning anything onto a child's garment. Since children will fiddle with the flower, they might hurt themselves with the point of a pin. Flowers can be attached to the ring bearer's ring pillow or sewn directly to the collar or belt of the flower girl's dress. This works very well if you are using silk flowers.

Flowers for Others

Some bridal couples may choose to honor family members who are not in the wedding party. Flowers are an easy way to do that. Mothers of the bride and groom are usually given corsages. Stepmothers may also get one, too. Fathers of the bride and groom are given boutonnieres, as well as stepfathers, especially if they have been close to the bridal couple. Grandmothers, grandfathers, siblings, aunts, and uncles sometimes are given flowers also. Be careful here. Try not to single out just one of these family members, unless everyone in the family knows how important that person is to you. Plan to give all of your aunts or sisters a corsage if you are thinking of giving a flower to only one.

Flowers for the Ceremony Location

Churches and Synagogues. Check with officials at the church or synagogue that you have booked. Find out if there are limitations on flower arrangement size or location.

Catholic churches do not permit anything, including wedding flowers, on the altar. Some Catholic churches don't want flowers anywhere in the area around the altar. Others want them to be seen from 360 degrees and should be placed on the floor and be no taller than the top of the altar. You can often place them on standing racks near the front of the church. They may also request that you leave your floral arrangements in the church for weekend masses.

Other churches will permit flowers everywhere, including on the altar itself, as well as at the end of each pew along with the pew bows.

In addition, many churches do not permit freestanding candelabras, floral arrangements with candles, or lamps. These are an added fire risk. If candles are permitted, they should be dripless or in hurricane globes.

Aisle runners may or may not be permitted in the church that you use. Bans on their use are due to the slope of the church and the potential risk of falling.

In some facilities, not just churches and synagogues, there is a prohibition on having the flower girl drop flower petals down the aisle. This makes for extra cleanup and could add to your facility rental fees.

Historical Locations. What you can place within these locations really depends on the policies of the site. Check with officials there about what is permitted.

Outdoors. Whether you wedding is in a public park, formal garden, or at Aunt Middy's farm, you usually can place a large flower arrangement somewhere near where the celebrant will be standing. These can be put on wire stands, in pots, or in baskets.

Resorts, Amusement Parks, etc. If your wedding is held at a resort, amusement park, or other destination, ask your contact there about ceremony flowers. That person should be able to let you know how many flowers you may use, their size, and where to place them.

Preparing Your Own Wedding Flowers

Though it can be a daunting task, making your own flowers is really an exciting option for some brides. Start planning at least two months before your wedding. Six to nine months before the ceremony is better. Allow yourself plenty of time for unforeseen events and to enjoy making the flowers.

Draft a list of how many bouquets, corsages, boutonnieres, and flower arrangements you will need. If the list seems too long and you don't want to cut it down, consider making only some of the items and having a florist do the others. For example, you enjoy doing table arrangements but think that making corsages and boutonnieres will be tedious. Then, contract out everything but the large floral arrangements.

Gather you materials as soon as you can so that you can begin working on the flowers as soon as possible. Make sure you have enough bouquet holders, plant oases, floral wire, corsage pins, floral tape, and ribbons in your wedding colors. Start looking for sources for your plant materials. You can find online suppliers of live flowers and greenery who are willing to ship directly to you. You can also find discount silk flower suppliers. Craft stores are also great places to find the items you need, including silk flowers and dried plant materials. You can also go out in the countryside and gather materials to dry.

Practice making some of the items early on. These mock-ups will act as guides for doing the rest. Try to make as much of your flower order as you can ahead of time. Sometimes, this is making floral ribbons and soaking floral oases in water. Items with live flowers and greenery can be put together as much as a week ahead of time. Store live plant materials in buckets of water. Put finished floral pieces in a cool place (under 50 degrees). Mist everyday and check on the water level often. Flowers in arrangements can last up to a week.

CHAPTER TEN

CHOOSING THE CEREMONY SITE AND CELEBRANT

Choosing the Ceremony Site

Today, couples can be married almost anywhere. Even in exotic or extreme situations as in a skydiving wedding, couples can tie the knot wherever they want. It may take some persistence, some cash, and some insider influence, but it can be done. If you are willing to create your dream wedding, plan well and stay positive.

Many brides are choosing to hold the ceremony at the same site as the reception. This eliminates someone getting lost between the ceremony and the party. It also can trim your wedding costs because there is only one rental fee and only one location to decorate. In some cases, the wedding participants and their guests just move to another part of the location. There is one room that is set up for the ceremony and another room for the reception. Some venues will set up for the ceremony in part of a large room and then set up for the reception while the guests greet the wedding party through a leisurely receiving line and then a pause at the bar.

Special Needs

Determining your wedding style will help you decide where to hold your wedding ceremony. When these early decisions are made, you can then book your ceremony location. Whatever you decide, make sure that your location is accessible. This is especially important if the bridal couple, members of the wedding party, or invited guests have mobility issues. Make sure that everyone can get to your wedding ceremony location and the site for the reception, without having to hire 300-pound linebackers to lift Uncle Harry's wheelchair all the way up the fifty stone steps in front of the building.

Most public places now must comply with Americans with Disabilities Act codes. These facilities will usually have ramps or elevators on site as well as wheelchair accessible bathrooms. Unfortunately, many historic buildings may not have these accommodations due to the nature of preserving their historic value.

Another consideration is whether any of the guests or members of the wedding party have hearing problems. Sometimes, just having microphones surrounding the celebrant and the bridal couple lets everyone hear those precious vows and words of support coming from the celebrant.

Some churches, large hotels, and convention centers have deaf interpreters on staff or they can connect you with those that they use. If you are using another location, you can usually find interpreters for the deaf through disability support services at universities, local social service agencies, or disability groups in your community. There will be an extra fee for this service, but it will enhance your wedding day when you know that everyone can understand the beautiful readings, songs, and vows you have selected for your special day.

Churches and Synagogues

If you are planning a religious service, your decision about the site of your ceremony may be very simple. Just call your church or synagogue and book a date. If you aren't using your local church, your options broaden but may be complicated by a number of factors.

It isn't always easy to book another church or to ask a minister to do the honors outside of his own congregation. If you don't belong to a church and don't know a minister personally and still want to be married in a religious ceremony, finding a celebrant and a site to hold your wedding may be more difficult. Some churches are so busy that they cannot book weddings for people who are not members of their churches. Others refuse unless you become members or take instruction. Still others just won't do it because they don't rent out their sanctuary. In addition, though some ministers will consider marrying a non-member couple, they won't do it in their church building unless their congregation is invited.

Churches and synagogues, however, are not the only places to have a religious ceremony. This is where creativity and inventiveness come into play. Some of the locations for your wedding ceremony can be fraternal lodges, clubs, hotels, restaurants, gardens, historic buildings, and private homes. You could also use a public park, formal garden, hotel, country club, or restaurant. Almost any location, indoors or out, can serve as your ceremony site. The complication is finding a proper celebrant.

If you choose to hold both your ceremony and reception at a church, you will need to find out whether the alcohol you want to serve is permitted on church property and whether the music you want at your wedding reception is acceptable in the church's or synagogue's hall. For example, a chamber orchestra or a harpist might be perfect in any location, but a rock band pounding out Arrowsmith tunes may not fit a very conservative church's clientele. Church and synagogue halls often are set up by church volunteers, unless your caterers will do that for you. Therefore, keeping on the good graces of the church ladies may be to your best advantage.

Once you decide on the church or synagogue of your choice, call the church office and book an appointment with the minister, priest, or rabbi. Discuss your plans for your wedding and see if the church and the celebrant are free on the date you request. Some churches have wedding coordinators who work with couples to make their weddings go smoothly and to make sure they are conducted according to church protocols. You may be required to schedule an appointment with the wedding coordinator.

Some churches give the couple a special wedding booklet that answers many of your questions about decorations, lighting, photographs, music, and the wedding service itself. It also lists fees for everything from the celebrant's fee, the church rental, and the wedding coordinator's fee. Use fees can run from $100 for the church and hall all the way up to $2,000 or more just for the church. Variation in fees depends on the size of the church and whether the church is located in a large metropolitan area. Wedding coordinator fees range from $50 to $200.

Lodges and Halls

Nearly every town has a VFW, American Legion, Knights of Columbus, Elks Hall or Masonic Lodge. There are many other fraternal and service organizations that offer their facilities to members' families or to the community at large. These organizations are good places to hold either the ceremony or the reception, or both.

Like religious halls, you will need to find out what is provided, such as tables and chairs, who will set up and clean up, and what kinds of decorations they will permit. Some of these facilities, especially Masonic Temples or Lodges, have beautifully appointed halls with dance floors, raised platform areas, and big kitchens. They can be set up into aisles just like a church. The cost for rental can run from $300 on up.

Clubs, Hotels, and Restaurants

Many hotels and fine restaurants have separate banquet rooms that can be used for your ceremony and reception. Banquet coordinators at hotels and restaurants are very skilled in wedding planning and can give you much needed advice. Just remember, though, that they are representing their facility's kitchen and may push to sell their site as your reception location as well. If the menu and costs are within your wedding budget and correspond to your wedding style, it may be a great choice.

Costs can range from a few hundred dollars to thousands, depending on whether the facility provides catering or not. Some small restaurants can be rented out for an entire evening. Costs can be competitive with a banquet facility that provides catering.

Private Homes and Gardens

Having your wedding ceremony and reception at your parent's home may allow you more flexibility and more opportunity to do things your way. However, though the site may be free, costs can start to add up if you are renting tents, tables, linens, etc. You will need to determine whether the location will accommodate all of your guests and whether there is adequate guest parking. You will also need to provide sufficient bathroom facilities for your guests. That may involve renting portable toilets. Additionally, you will need to look at your lighting needs, especially if you are holding your ceremony and reception outside after dark.

If the reception is not possible, the wedding ceremony itself could be held in the backyard or garden of your home or the home of a good friend. If you are planning a small wedding, this is a good option. You could even have the ceremony inside if there is room enough.

Someone we know had her ceremony at the church in her small town, but had the reception in a renovated barn on the bride's grandparent's property. Since the town was so small, the whole town came out for the ceremony and the reception.

Finally, you will need to notify your neighbors that you will be having a wedding and reception on a particular day. In some towns, you will need to get a noise variance for your reception so that your guests' laughter and your wedding reception music doesn't cause your neighbors to call the police. People often get noise variances for block parties, and since all of the neighbors are invited, there usually isn't a problem.

Costs may be free for the site, but rentals and extra serving or parking help may add up.

Public Facilities: Gardens, Museums, and Historic Homes

Public facilities can be quite inexpensive for a wedding ceremony. Call your local Historical Society or Chamber of Commerce for suggestions about historic buildings, private mansions, wineries, or art galleries. City, county, and state facilities are also good wedding possibilities. These can include state or county parks (some have nice lodges), university or college facilities, castles, museums, libraries, public gardens, and marinas.

Costs can begin to mount as well as complications about permissions to use the facilities when you plan a reception at these sites. Liability issues are given most often. There is concern about guests' welfare, as well as the integrity of the site itself. Having a big wedding dance with a rock band and lots of messy food and drink could put off curators of museums, causing them to worry about the safety of the art displayed or the facility itself. When you are dealing with food and drink, there always is spillage and breakage.

In contrast, a wedding ceremony just involves seating, flowers, music, and people. Most people responsible for renting public facilities usually don't have issues with wedding ceremonies.

What to Check Out

Always visit the ceremony site before you make a final decision. Make sure you see the actual room where the ceremony will be held and ask lots of questions.

Ask about room capacity or how many people the room will accommodate. Many public facilities are bound by fire codes and have restrictions on how many people can be in the facility at any given time.

Look for windows and lighting. Find out if there is one part of the room that would be a good focal point to be a good background for the ceremony activities. Examine the décor of the facility to make sure it is in keeping with your wedding theme. Find out if you will need to bring in extra decorations to enhance your theme and if that is permitted.

Discuss any restrictions with the contact person at the facility. Find out if the building is non-smoking. Are you permitted to use candles? Can you use rice or confetti on the facility grounds? Are there restrictions on music within the building? If the bride and groom will be sharing a cup of wine or other drink during the ceremony, find out if alcohol is permitted or if you can bring in liquids. This is a crucial question in an historical location or in a museum.

Also inquire about extra tables for wedding gifts or the guest book. Ask about a PA system if the facility is large and you are concerned about everyone hearing what the celebrant says. If a PA isn't available, ask whether you can bring in a small one. Check on the bathroom facilities and whether there is enough parking.

Finally, check to see if the facility is available for the date you want. Find out what other events will be taking place at the facility on your wedding day. This will let you know whether you will have enough time to set up and remove decorations and flowers. You will also have a better idea of whether you will be rushed to vacate the premises.

Equally important, if you are planning on using the facility for your reception, you will need to ask questions about that. (Please see the checklists in our two companion books: *The Ultimate Wedding Reception Book* and *The Ultimate Wedding Workbook*.)

Rental Fees and Deposits

Nearly all facilities have rental fees and usually require a deposit. Before you sign a contract, make sure you know what you are paying for. Is the fee based on an hourly rate or for a block of time? What is included at the facility—chairs, decorations, etc.? Is there a fee if you don't vacate the facility on time? Does the fee include taxes and gratuities?

Find out what the deposit is and when it must be paid. Usually, deposits are paid at the time you sign your contract or rental agreement. Sometimes, deposits are amounts paid in addition to the rental fees. The deposit acts not only as a sign of commitment but also as a damage fee. Find out when you must pay the balance of the rental fee.

Choosing the Celebrant

The person who officiates your wedding can be almost anyone recognized by the state in which you live to perform marriages. In most cases, that person is a minister, priest, rabbi, or other religious leader authorized by a religious body. The celebrant can also be a justice of the peace. In some cases, justices happen to also be city mayors or other elected officials. It depends on what the rules are for your state. Some states are very liberal and others are very strict.

Often times, justices of the peace only marry couples at city hall or the county court house. Sometimes, they will agree to go to another location to marry someone they know.

Some ministers, especially family friends, can be brought in from other states or cities to marry couples. Oftentimes, this happens at facilities other than churches. Although, some minister friends have been brought in to marry couples at university churches since the students come from different parts of the country. Some Unitarian Universalist Churches will sometimes permit other clergy to marry couples in their churches, and their clergy or designated wedding celebrants have been known to marry couples that aren't members of their own congregations. This varies from congregation to congregation.

If you don't know a minister personally and you don't want to be married at city hall, you can check out wedding chapels. They are appearing more and more in places other than Las Vegas and Reno. Usually, the celebrant is a retired justice or minister. Sometimes, the celebrant has obtained a state license by an affiliation with the Universal Life Church or other mail-order ministerial agency. Such documentation is recognized by some states and makes the wedding legal. In fact, though a public ceremony is conducted by a licensed person, the thing that makes the marriage legal in many states is the marriage license, duly signed by the celebrant, the couple, and two witnesses.

Other places to find a celebrant is by asking friends, looking in the yellow pages for wedding chapels, asking wedding vendors who they would recommend, and even the Internet. There are licensed wedding celebrants in many states who craft unique wedding ceremonies for people who want a spiritual slant but not a religious one.

Whoever you choose to officiate your wedding, ask about their credentials to make sure they are legal in your state. Then, ask lots of questions to see if the celebrant is a good fit for your ceremony.

Religious Obligations

One addition to your wedding ceremony planning is wedding preparation classes. Some states offer a discount on your wedding license for attendance in these classes, which are usually offered by churches or family service agencies for a fee. These classes deal with finances, the legalities of marriage, problem solving, and intimacy issues.

Some churches require a couple's active participation in marriage instruction classes. Involving several sessions, these classes can take several weeks. Some churches require that they be completed before the ceremony can be booked in the church. In this case, you will need to take this time lag into consideration as you plan.

In addition, Catholic churches must issues the banns, announcing your upcoming marriage in their church bulletins and from the pulpit. This is done for three consecutive weeks before the wedding. It's an old custom, allowing everyone to know about the marriage and give anyone who has reason to do so to object to the marriage.

CHAPTER ELEVEN

WHAT'S IN A CEREMONY?

Ceremony Basics

A wedding ceremony has one basic part: the exchange of vows. No matter the type of ceremony, whether religious, ethnic, or secular, all marriages have vows of commitment. That's the purpose of the wedding. The flowers, the rings, the prayers, the blessings, and everything else just reinforce those pledges of commitment. All of the wedding ceremony embellishments vary according to the experience and backgrounds of the couple.

Some sample ceremony outlines for religious, secular, and ethic or cultural ceremonies will help you decide what you want to include in your own ceremony. For some religious couples, you many not have much leeway in deciding what elements you want to include in your wedding service. Other couples may have the opportunity and freedom to write their own services. In every case, couples can choose particular readings and vows for their wedding ceremonies.

Religious Ceremonies

The order of service for religious weddings varies not only from religion to religion but also from church to church.

Catholic. The Catholic wedding, steeped in old traditions and beautiful rituals, is probably the most structured wedding ceremony in America. Because most Catholic marriages include a Mass, the wedding service lasts an hour or more, slightly longer than a regular Catholic Mass.

There are a few opportunities for couples to add their voices to the Liturgy of Marriage. They may select readings, vows, and hymns from a booklet they received at Pre-Cana or Marriage Encounter classes. These booklets are usually printed by St. Anthony Messenger Press and offer a variety of wedding selections.

The Processional. Both bride and groom enter down the center aisle, often with family members.

The Introductions/Liturgy of the Word. The priest greets the congregation and begins with a prayer. A reading from the Old Testament and a responsorial psalm are given by readers chosen by the couple. The priest offers the Gospel reading and gives a short homily on marriage.

Vows/Exchange of Rings. The whole congregation stands as the couple exchanges their vows. Usually the priest asks the questions and the couple responds with the traditional, "I do." Then the priest takes the rings and blesses each one before passing it to the bride or groom to put on the other person's finger. The bride and groom each say a commitment as they place the ring on each other's fingers. Sometimes, this is prompted by the priest who has the couple repeat what he says.

Mass. This is a full worship and communion service. Some couples are opting to just have a wedding service and not a mass.

Benedictory Prayer. This is prayer of blessing on the couple and the congregation.

Recessional. The bride and groom return up the aisle, with the wedding party following. The congregation follows as ushers signal their departure pew by pew.

You will note that Unity candles are not part of a Catholic wedding.

Protestant. Most Protestant denominations follow the same basic format, though there will be a lot of variation on what might be included as extras. For example, Seventh Day Adventists don't exchange rings. There can be many additions to the basic service.

The Processional. The groom usually waits at the altar with the groomsmen and the minister. Sometimes, the groomsmen come down the aisle, paired with the bridesmaids. Some grooms choose to process down the aisle with his family.

Introduction/Welcome. The minister welcomes the congregation and announces the intention of the service. He says a variation of: "We are gathered her to witness the marriage of Susan and John in holy matrimony." The minister then says a prayer and asks, "Who brings this woman to be married to this man?" Instead of this, some ministers will simply ask if both families approve of the marriage and pledge their support. The families respond in either case.

Vows/Exchange of Rings. Many Protestant denominations now not only approve but also encourage couples to write their own vows. They should all have some sort of permanence stated in them. The rings are also exchanged with the bride and groom each saying, "This ring I give you in token of our abiding love," or a variation. This can be also be reworded to fit the couple's sense of poetry and romance.

Unity Candle Ceremony. This is a phenomenon of Protestant weddings. A large wedding candle called a unity candle represents the couple's commitment. As a song is sung, the bride and groom each light a single candle, and then together they light the unity candle.

Benediction/Exit. The minister may say The Lord's Prayer or a special benediction prayer. He pronounces the bride and groom husband and wife. The couple kisses. Often, the minister then has the couple face the congregation, and he introduces them as Mr. and Mrs. The congregation usually applauds and this signals the couple's departure up the aisle, with the wedding party following.

Jewish. A Jewish wedding takes place under a wedding canopy called a *huppah*. This lovely tradition began during the Middle Ages when marriages were held outdoors under the stars. This was supposed to ensure that the wedding couple would be blessed with many children, as many as the stars in the sky.

Before the couple meets under the huppah, there are a couple of other important traditions. Before the wedding, the groom tries to give a talk on the week's Torah lesson to the men in the congregation. The game here is that they try their utmost to interrupt him. In another room, the bride is doing the same thing. Both the bride and groom are permitted to do this together in liberal congregations.

Unlike Christian weddings where the marriage license is signed after the wedding, the *Ketubah* or marriage contract is signed before the wedding. The *Ketubah* is a visually beautiful document, which describes the promises, rights, and responsibilities of a married couple under Jewish law. In Orthodox congregations, only the men sign the contract, but in Conservative and Reformed Judaism congregations, both the bride and groom, the rabbi, and the witnesses sign it. The *Ketubah* is eventually hung in the couple's home.

In Orthodox marriages, there is one more pre-wedding tradition, the *b'deken*. Here the groom finds the bride who is surrounded by both families and covers the bride's face with her veil. This symbolizes the groom's choosing her and loving her inner beauty.

A Jewish wedding has three main sections.

The Processional and Circling. The bride and groom process to the *huppah*. When they enter the canopy, the groom circles the bride seven times. This symbolizes the seven days of creation, the seven wedding blessings, and the groom's love for his bride. In Conservative or Reformed congregations, both the bride and the groom circle each other.

Vows/Ring Exchange or *Kiddushin*. Traditionally, the groom will recite an ancient Aramaic vow as he puts the ring on the index finger of her right hand. Then, the bride does the same, if it is a double-ring ceremony. Many congregations are bowing to Western custom and placing the rings on the third finger of the left hand.

Blessings or *Sheva B'rachot*. The seven wedding blessings are read by the rabbi or a close family friend. These blessing include peace in the Holy Land, luck for the bride and groom, and praises to God. Then, the groom smashes a wine glass wrapped in a cloth with his foot. (This has many different meanings. Some say it represents the destruction of the temple in Jerusalem, and others say it shows how easy it is to break someone's heart. Most rabbis seem to think that it shows how marriage changes lives in a very permanent way.) The congregation shouts, "Mazel Tov!" (congratulations), and the couple and the guests head for the reception.

Non-Religious Ceremony

A wedding is a public commitment of a couple, pledging to build a life together. Many people choose to include their religious beliefs, traditions, and support systems in that commitment. The church family becomes the body that affirms and encourages the couple's life together. Many other couples have difficulty with organized religion, yet may feel deeply about the world and about their commitment to each other. These couples may choose a non-religious wedding ceremony and craft it in such a way to communicate their individuality and their sense of commitment.

A non-religious wedding ceremony is not confined to religious tradition or the use of scripture. However, it can be romantic, meaningful, and often deeply spiritual. Much of the order of the non-religious ceremony is the same as for the religious wedding.

Spiritual. A spiritual, non-religious wedding will reflect the couple's individual choices in readings, music, and even what the celebrant says about marriage. Though religious language is not used and even God may not be named, the feel of the wedding is still one of sacredness and deep, personal commitment. God may be called the Creator, the Divine, or Spirit, or some other non-gendered, non-parental term.

Secular poets and readings may be used in the ceremony. Earth elements may also be used. For example, if you are doing a seaside wedding, you might want to pour sand into a bowl instead of lighting a unity candle. For a sunrise wedding, your vows could reflect new beginnings with each dawn.

Often, these weddings take a lot of thought and planning. Sometimes, they are totally written by the bridal couple or co-written with the celebrant.

Secular. Secular weddings are usually briefer that any other wedding ceremony. They deal with the basics: greeting, vows, rings, kiss, and pronouncement of man and wife. These are the kind justices of the peace often do. There may be a poem or two in the wedding service about love. They are just as legal as any other kind of wedding and can be very beautiful.

Writing Your Own

Many couples today are writing their own wedding ceremonies. You can do that, too. Just gather a few examples of wedding services to get ideas. You can find them on the Internet or by asking clergymen to give you copies of different wedding services that they use. Once you have a few ideas in mind, draft an outline of the service and then plug in your ideas.

Some couples like to create special moments to honor their parents. They could have each mother bring a flower arrangement to place on the altar before the service. If the bridal couple will share a cup of wine during the service, each mother could pour a bit of wine from a bottle into the cup, symbolizing the merging of two households, two families. We know of one couple who did this right before the service, as the celebrant read a short litany of family surnames, connecting the couple not just with each other's immediate families but a glimpse of their entire lineages. You could do that with most any substance to show the blending of two families. This is an especially good idea for encore couples to show the merging of two households.

Whatever that you find important can be expressed in your wedding ceremony. Just use your imagination and create something special for your wedding.

CHAPTER TWELVE

POETRY OF THE HEART: CEREMONY READINGS

How Many Readings?

There really is no limit to the number of readings you can have in your wedding ceremony. You do, of course, need to be mindful of the length of your ceremony and any religious requirements you will need to follow. These will guide you in selecting your readings.

Generally, there are two to three scripture readings for a religious service. Some church weddings combine inspirational poetry or readings with scripture. For a non-religious service, you can have up to five readings, if they are short.

As you think about readings for your wedding, make sure that what you select fits your personality and how you and your groom feel about each other. Don't just choose readings that are popular or might appear to be romantic or lofty-sounding. Sometimes, the simplest poetry or prose is very effective and can be highly moving in a wedding service.

Finding Readers

When selecting readers, make sure that each person has a pleasant voice and can read well. Your wedding may not be Hollywood with professional voice talent, but you will want your readings to be clearly heard and understood. You also will want your guests to feel the impact of each precious word that you have chosen. Try to suit each reading with the reader's voice and personality if you can.

Some possible choices for readers are members of your wedding party, especially the best man or maid/matron of honor. Many couples ask friends or relatives who aren't in the wedding party to be readers. Sometimes, the parents of the bride and groom read something or a special aunt or uncle is chosen to read. On occasion, the bride or groom or both choose to do a reading.

If you have readers who have trouble reading small print, there is a way to accommodate them. Many people who have difficulty reading small type usually will print out reading materials in a larger font. As a courtesy to these readers, discuss the reading print size with your readers when you meet with them to give them their assigned readings. You could print out all of the readings yourself, according to the needs of these readers, and distribute them on rehearsal night or right before the wedding.

Extra lighting is another simple fix for readers who have trouble reading small print. Discuss these needs with someone at the church, synagogue, or other ceremony location. Often a piano lamp or podium light will do the trick. A small, but bright, portable reading light like those used to read in bed can also be an easy solution.

Sometimes reading materials get lost before the wedding. Have someone from the wedding party bring all of your readings to the ceremony location the day of the service and distribute them to the readers or leave them on the podium for the readers to find. Try to chose someone who won't be running around like a chicken with his head cut off on the day of the wedding. A groomsman or usher is a good choice. Though they may have seating duties, they can make sure that this one segment of the wedding ceremony is in place.

Attractive Reading Materials

It is distracting to your guests if your readers are shuffling through tattered papers as they read. To make your readings extra special, print them out on cardstock or fancy parchment-like papers.

You can also put your readings in booklets with covers in your wedding colors.

Creating attractive reading materials shouldn't burden you or your wedding party. This could be a job for your high-tech nephew or your scrapbooking neighbor.

Reading Suggestions

There are beloved scripture readings that many couples choose time and again. These describe what love is, what a good husband or wife is, and the religious basis for marriage.

Scripture Readings

Old Testament New Testament
Genesis 1:26-31 Matthew 19:5-6
Genesis 2:18-24 Mark 10:6-9
Ruth: 16-17 John 2:1-12
Ruth 4 Romans 12:9-12
Proverbs 5: 15-19 I Corinthians 7
Proverbs 18:22 I Corinthians 11:3
Ecclesiastes 4:9-12 I Corinthians 11:8-9
Song of Solomon 2:10-13 I Corinthians 13:4-8 (the attributes of love)
Song of Solomon 8:6-7 II Corinthians 6:14
Jeremiah 31:31-34 Ephesians 3:14-19
Ephesians 4:9-12
Ephesians 5:22-33
Colossians 3:12-19
Hebrews 13:4
I Peter 3:1-7
I John 4:7-8
I John 4:12
Revelations 19:7-9

Inspirational readings and poetry describe love or convey blessings on the couple.

Inspirational Readings

"A History of Love"–Diane Ackerman

Excerpt from *Tuesdays with Morrie*–Mitch Albom

"A Marriage"–Author Unknown

Excerpt from *The Bridge Across Forever*–Richard Bach

"Sound of Silence"–Raymond J. Baughan

Excerpt from *The Country of Marriage*–Wendell Berry

"Friendship"–Judy Bielicki

"I Love You"–Roy Croft

"Blessing for a Marriage"–James Dillet Freeman

"On Marriage" from *The Prophet*–Kahlil Gibran

"On Love" from *The Prophet*–Kahlil Gibran

Excerpt from "Any Husband or Wife"–Carole Haynes

"Love Is Friendship Caught Fire"–Laura Hendricks

"Foundations of Marriage"–Regina Hill

"On Love"–Thomas a Kempis

Excerpt from *A Gift from the Sea*–Anne Morrow Lindbergh

"Marriage Joins Two People in the Circle of Its Love"–Edmund O'Neill

"Never Marry But for Love"–William Penn

Poetry Selections

"Touched by an Angel"–Maya Angelou
"How Do I Love Thee?"–Elizabeth Barrett Browning
"If Thou Must Love Me"–Elizabeth Barrett Browning
"She Walks in Beauty"–Lord Byron
"Love Lives"–John Clare
"My Love"–Linda Lee Elrod
"Bridal Song"–John Ford
"Marriage"–Mary Weston Fordham
"A New Beginning"–Gwen Frostic
"Fidelity"–D. H. Lawrence
"Sonnet LXIX"–Pablo Neruda
"Sudden Light"–Dante Gabriel Rosetti
"Love Is"–Susan Polis Schutz
"Sonnet 18"–William Shakespeare
"Sonnet 116"–William Shakespeare
"My True Love"–Sir Phillip Sydney

CHAPTER THIRTEEN

PLEDGING YOUR LOVE: CEREMONY VOWS AND BLESSINGS

Significance of Vows

Wedding vows are the centerpiece of the wedding ceremony. You can eliminate all of the frills of the ceremony—the flowers, the beautiful clothes, the music, and even the rings—but a wedding is not a wedding without the promises made between the bride and the groom. These promises of love and commitment are what a wedding is all about.

The bride and groom need to talk this over carefully. What you commit to each other shows how you view marriage and each other. Therefore, your content must express exactly what you are feeling toward each other. Select vows that come closest to how you feel about marriage and about your intended spouse.

Next decide on the format for the vows. Do you want to say the same things to each other? Do you want to memorize your vows or do you want to read them? An alternative is to have the celebrant say the vows you choose and you each respond with "I do" or "I will."

Suggested Vows

Here are some samples of different types of vows that couples have chosen to say at their weddings. Some are very old and some reflect the 21st century. Most vows have three questions that include the naming of the bride and groom and asking for the promise of marriage, asking for the extent of that commitment, and asking for some sense of permanence about that commitment.

> **Traditional Vows.** These vows are what your parents or grandparents said to each other. Some couples feel a connection to the past and with history when they use these vows.
>
> "Do you (groom/bride) take (bride/groom) to be your lawfully wedded wife/husband, to have and to hold from this day forward?"
>
> "I do."
>
> "Do you promise to love, honor, and cherish her/him for better or for worse, for richer or for poorer, in sickness and in health?"
>
> "I do."
>
> "And, forsaking all others, will you remain only unto her/him for as long as you both shall live?"
>
> "I do."

> **Modified Traditional Vows.** This set of vows has the three questions, but the last one adds a behavioral assurance.
>
> "(Groom/Bride) do you take (bride/groom), whom you now hold by the hand, to be your lawfully wedded wife/husband?"
>
> "I do."
>
> "Do you promise to love and cherish her/him in sickness and in health, for richer, for poorer, for better, for worse, and forsaking all others keep yourself only unto her/him, for as long as you both shall live."
>
> "I do."

"Do you mutually promise in the presence of your friends and family that you will at all times and in all circumstances, conduct yourselves toward one another as becomes a husband and a wife?"

"We do."

Modern Vows. New vows are offering couples the opportunity to speak their hearts. These new vows talk of friendship and equal partners, support and working together. Modern vows pack a lot of punch in a few words. Often the questions are lumped together and the bride or groom answers them all together.

"(Groom/Bride) do you pledge to love, honor, and cherish (bride/groom), and throughout your years together be honest, faithful, and kind to her/him? Do you pledge to give her/him the same happiness she/he gives to you, to react to her/him as only you can, and to respect her/him for who she/he is, not who you want her/him to be?"

"I do."

Proclamation Vows. These are very public, personal commitments to each other. There are no questions. There are only statements of commitment.

"With all my heart, I take you, (name), to be my wife/husband. I will love you through the good and the bad, through the joy and the sorrow. I will try to be understanding and to trust in you completely. I will make you a part of me and in turn become a part of you. Together we will face all of life's experiences and share one another's dreams and goals. We will be equal partners in an open and honest relationship throughout the years."

Intentional Vows. These just show the intent or willingness to commit to another person. They reflect a realistic view of working on a relationship.

"(Groom/Bride) it is my intention to be your best friend, to respect and support you, to be patient with you, to work together with you to achieve those things that are important to us, to accept you unconditionally, and to share life with you throughout the years."

Pledged Vows. These are like intentional vows, in that they are statements not responses to questions.

"(Groom/Bride), I pledge to you with all my heart and being to love and support you in all ways to my utmost capabilities for the rest of our days."

Encore Vows. When you marry again, your vows should reflect the life experience you now have. Creative encore vows are some of the most romantic vows written. Here are some beautiful examples.

"I marry you with open eyes. Because of you, I laugh again and dare to dream.

Together, we have let go of the past and now look toward the future. I give you my love, my heart, and my willingness to build a life with you. I promise to bring you joy and to learn to love you more each day."

"We have been given a second chance at happiness. I thank God that I found you. My love for you is endless and eternal. As we begin to build a life together, I offer you my faithfulness and trust. I promise to care for you, to nurture you, and to make you laugh often."

For the older couple remarrying, your wedding vows can be extra special.

"I offer you the autumn of my life. I promise to be a companion worthy of your precious friendship. As our life together begins, I pledge to welcome your loving family and your dear friends into a wide circle of care and support. Though we cherish the memories of the past, we will create new ones in our life together."

Sometimes, couples include a children's vow after their formal vows are said. The children are asked the following questions and they respond, "We do." If you chose to use such a vow, make sure that your children are happy about your remarriage. You don't want to embarrass yourself or the children at the church if they loudly yell, "No!"

"And now, (children's names) do you promise to love and respect your parent's new husband/wife? Do you promise to support their marriage and their new family? Do you promise to accept the responsibility of being their children, and to encourage them and support them in your new life together?"

Writing Your Own

In many ceremonies, the bride and groom choose to craft promises to each other that reflect their personalities and the depth of their commitment to each other. Before you head for the computer, sit down and talk about the structure of your vows. Do you want to say different things or to say the same lines? There is a symmetry and consistency in having the bride and groom say the same words. However, it is often more interesting to hear words that express different aspects of the couple's relationship. Next, decide on the length of your vows. Usually, they're only four or five sentences.

You will need to take some time to think about what your fiancé means to you. Think back about when you first met. Make a list of the qualities that you love about your fiancé. Think about the qualities that you believe make a marriage strong. Think about the qualities that you have shown that support your fiancé. Also, consider what you are comfortable saying in front of a group of people.

When you have given all of this thought, you will be ready to write your own vows. Don't be afraid to alter them or amend them as you think about your marriage. When you are content with the wording, practice reading them. Also, consider reading them to each other before the wedding. This will prepare both of you for what is said and will allow you to react emotionally when the two of you are alone. Put your vows on small cards and read from them on the day of your wedding.

New Promises for the Rings

In place of the traditional "With this ring, I thee wed" and its variations, many modern couples are opting to use different wording as an echo or addition to their vows. Variations on this theme are: "With this ring, I pledge my love," "With this ring, I pledge my commitment," "With this ring, I pledge my love and commitment."

The following promise is one of the new ones used as wedding rings are exchanged.

"With this ring, I give you my promise that from this day forward we shall walk together through all that life puts before us. May my heart be your shelter and my arms be your home."

Wedding Blessings

These special blessings may be read as is or altered to suit your particular circumstances. That is the beauty of writing or editing your own vows and blessings because it builds in versatility and makes these special moments very personal. Most couples use these wedding blessings as benedictions.

Apache Blessing. Many couples use this entire blessing or just the first part of it.

Apache Blessing

Now you will feel no rain,
For each of you will be shelter to the other.
Now you will feel no cold,
For each of you will be warmth to the other.
Now there is no more loneliness for you.
For each of you will be companion to the other.

Now you are two bodies,
But there is only one life before you.
Go now to your dwelling place,
To enter into the days of your togetherness
And may your days be good and long upon the earth.
Treat yourselves and each other with respect,
And remind yourselves often of what brought you together.
Give the highest priority to the tenderness, gentleness,
And kindness that your connection deserves.

Unity Candle Blessings. Many couples like the idea of providing a visual symbol of uniting two people's lives in marriage. One popular symbol is the unity candle. The parents of the bride light individual tapers before the wedding starts. Usually, after the vows and the exchange of rings, the bride and groom take the individual candles and light a large unity candle, symbolizing the commitment of one life together. Sometimes, the grandparents or the bride's and groom's children from a previous marriage light the individual candles. On occasion, the children of encore couples light individual candles of their own and help the bride and groom light the big unity candle.

Harold Douglas's poem is often recited by the celebrant during the lighting of the unity candle. Other celebrants extend the candle lighting moment through additional readings, but many use a variation of the blessing below.

"Today, (bride) and (groom) make a loving commitment to follow the greatest Commandment of all: Love one another, as I have loved you." They do this in hope that their union will become a symbol of God's promise to merge two lives into one.

"The two distinct flames represent your lives to this moment; individual and unique. As you light the center candle together, the entwined rings symbolize your two lives joined in dependence and growing maturity. Your plans will be mutual, your joys and sorrows will be shared alike. May the light of this unity candle warm your new life together and brighten all your days."

Blessing of the Hands. This beautiful blessing is creating its own niche in the wedding ceremony. It is read by the maid/matron of honor and the best man. It is extremely emotional, especially if the maid/matron of honor and the best man are married and appear to be giving the bride and groom special advice from their years of marriage. It usually is read before the vows are said.

Maid/matron of honor reads:

(Bride), please face (groom) and hold his hands, palms up, so you may see the gift that they are to you. These are the hands, young and strong and vibrant with love, that are holding yours on your wedding day, as he promises to love you all the days of his life. These are the hands that will gently stroke your brow when you are tense or tired. These are the hands that will wipe the tears of joy and sorrow from your eyes. These are the hands that will hold onto you through difficult times. These are the hands that will support you as you follow your dreams. These are the hands that will passionately love you and cherish you through the years, for a lifetime of happiness.

Best Man reads:

(Groom), please hold (bride's) hands, palms up, so you may see the gift that they are to you. These are the hands, smooth and young, that are holding yours on your wedding day, as she promises to love you all the days of her life. These are the hands that will massage the tension from your neck and back in the evenings after you've both had a long, hard day. These are the hands that will hold onto you through difficult times. These are the hands that will comfort you when you are sick or comfort you when you are grieving. These are the hands that will support you as you follow your dreams. These are the hands that will passionately love you and cherish you through the years, for a lifetime of happiness.

Celebrant reads:

Bless the hands that you see before you this day. May they always be held by each other. Give them the strength to hold on during the storms of stress and the dark of disillusionment. Keep them tender and gentle as they nurture each other in their love. Help these hands continue building a relationship together, rich in grace, in caring, and in devotion.

CHAPTER FOURTEEN

SINGING THE HEART: CEREMONY MUSIC

Music is very much a part of our daily lives and therefore an integral part of our special celebrations. We listen to music at work and in the car. We listen to music to relax us and to energize us. We listen to music to find stillness within and to worship. Therefore, making decisions about music for a wedding ceremony is vital to creating the mood that you want for your wedding. It is important to remember your wedding style and theme when finalizing your music plans.

Recorded Music or Live Musicians?

There are five main issues to think about when deciding about using recorded music or live musicians. They are ambiance, site limitations or restrictions, musical taste, intent, and budget. All of these considerations may be intertwined or distinct in your planning.

Ambiance. Ambiance is tied in with your wedding style and theme. If you are planning an island theme or Cajun wedding, you may want Cajun music, a reggae song, or maybe a steel drum group. If you are planning an elegant formal wedding, a flutist or a small chamber orchestra might be ideal. A big band or roaring twenties theme might suggest using music from that era. For a medieval wedding or an ethnic theme, you might want to use madrigal singers, a harpist, or ethnic musicians.

Venue limitations. Venue limitations to consider are physical size of the space and venue restrictions or rules. You will need to find out where within the space you can put musicians or singers. If you are using recorded music, you will need to inquire whether the facility has an audio system or whether you will need to rent one. Venues cannot tell you how many musicians or singers to hire or how much equipment they should bring, but they can give you information about the space and other events at the facility on your wedding day that will help you make your decision. Churches have their own sets of rules and can restrict not only the number of musicians but also the kind of music you select. They can tell you that they have space restrictions and noise ordinances. Find out what they are before you sign the contract to rent the facility.

Musical taste. Your wedding theme and your personal taste in music will ultimately determine what music you choose. Try to be consistent with your wedding theme, if possible. You don't want to have the latest Shania Twain song sung at a medieval wedding, nor would you want a bagpiper for a Roman theme wedding. Notwithstanding, some churches don't want any secular music used in wedding ceremonies.

Intent. Whatever music you choose for your wedding should not only be in keeping with your wedding style and theme, but it also should enhance your wedding ceremony. Each musical selection should reflect what you are saying in your vows and in the readings you choose. So, take your time in selecting ceremony music. Listen to a lot of tracks. Get copies of the lyrics and read them. Make a list of songs that fit our criteria. Then, select only those songs that that will make your wedding perfect.

Budget. Generally, couples spend about 9% of their wedding budget on music for both the ceremony and the reception. For a $25,000 wedding, that comes to $2,250. The majority of that budget usually goes to the reception entertainment. You may decide to spend more on the ceremony music if you are doing a small reception, such as a cake and punch affair. As a rule, recorded music is less expensive than live musicians, unless they are friends or relatives who are giving you their musical talents as a wedding gift.

Plan your music budget early on. Don't let it be just a last minute figure that you get after you budget for everything else. You might find that you don't have much money left over. When you start looking for a soloist or an organist, you might be stuck with getting somebody less experienced or with less talent.

Equipment. Consider equipment when you are looking at your wedding budget and the limitations of the venue. If you are using live musicians, find out if they have their own equipment or must rent it. Determine exactly what their power needs will be. You don't want your musicians to be snaking power cords all over the church or the banquet hall. Make sure that the musicians aren't bringing in more power than the room can handle. For example, if you have booked a small banquet hall and the musicians start carting in six-foot outdoor Marshal stacks, you know that your great-aunt Bertha will be blown out of her wheelchair and plastered against the back wall. Don't let that be a wedding day surprise. Go see the musicians play live.

You also don't want a huge pile of speakers and instrument cases marring your guests' view of your wedding ceremony. Make sure that the equipment they use is in good working condition. You don't want to hear hiss or buzz during the music or popping or roaring when people speak into the microphone. Find out if the musicians have a backup plan in case something happens to their equipment.

If it matters to you how your wedding soloists or musicians look, there are some remedies. Some usage wear on equipment is unavoidable, especially if the musician or singer tours extensively. Most music professionals take pride in the state of their equipment and will try to fix many of the more unsightly dents and dings. However, if there are offensive stickers or slogans on the musicians' PA equipment, you might want to either ask them to cover them during the ceremony or not hire the musicians in the first place.

Make sure that your soloists and musicians visit the ceremony site with you. Have them discuss their power needs with the venue. People in charge at the facility, such as hall managers and wedding coordinators, might also be able to help with personnel or referrals to equipment rental companies that might be able to solve a particular problem.

Live Musicians and Soloists

Choosing the right soloist or musician can be a challenge. As we've talked about before, you need to match the performer with your wedding theme, the time of day of your wedding, the size of the ceremony site, and your budget. Ask your friends and relatives for suggestions. Remember, though, that a performer seen in one setting may not have the same feel in another, especially in the formality of a wedding service.

Draft a list of potential musicians and soloists. Find out where they are playing and go listen. If the performer sings in church, go to a service and take notes. If the performer plays regularly in clubs or coffeehouses, ask the venue owner about details. Find out how reliable the performer is, who he or she has played with, and where else have the performer played. Look at the appearance of the performer. Will that image fit in with your guests or your theme? What is the state of the equipment?

If you can't go see the musician or soloist live, find out a contact number and call the performer. Ask for a demo to listen to. Remember, though, that with state-of-the-art studio equipment that can blip out sour notes and wrong chords, you might be listening to quite a different performer than what he or she is like live. Also, find out whether any members of a musical group have been replaced since the CD. Then, try to find out where they are playing and go see them live.

In your dialogue with the performer, ask about experience, training, and references. Find out from references if the performer takes a lot of smoke breaks or heads for the bar at every available moment. Ask what others have done about food and beverage privileges for this particular performer for receptions and wedding ceremonies. Though you are hiring someone for the ceremony, it is a courtesy to ask him or her to attend the reception. Find out if the performer has abused the open bar privilege or eaten all of the leftover cake.

Find out what the performer's attire is and whether he or she would consider more formal dress for your wedding. Ask if the musician or soloist would be willing to dress in garments that fit your theme.

Ask about the fee. For a wedding ceremony, which is under an hour, the performer will probably only do one or two musical selections and won't take any breaks. Find out if the performer expects travel expenses to be included. Usually, the performer's fee is a set rate, period.

Find out when the performer can load into the facility and load out. Some halls, churches, and historical buildings will allow wedding participants and vendors to come in about an hour or two before the wedding and want the facility cleared a half hour to an hour afterwards. Find out if the performer can set up, do their sound check, and break down and load out within this time frame. Ask about any illness or cancellation policy that the performer has. Would a musical group be willing to replace performers or bring in a backup group if they couldn't make it due to car breakdown or illness? Make sure you sign a detailed contract with all contingencies laid out.

Recorded Music

Sometimes a wedding DJ will help with recorded music for the ceremony, especially processional and recessional music. The wedding DJ may also provide prelude music. If you engage a wedding DJ to do your wedding ceremony music, make sure that the facility, especially a church, approves of recorded music for weddings. Usually, a wedding DJ is asked to do the ceremony music if he or she has been hired to do the music for the reception. It is rare that a wedding DJ would do a wedding and not the reception as well. Please keep that in mind as you investigate this option. After all, wedding DJs will be moving in a sound system and lots of music and will need time to set up and take down.

To find a good wedding DJ, go through the same process as finding a live performer. Get recommendations from friends and family, especially those recently married. Ask your caterer or reception facility for suggestions. Go to bridal showcases or wedding expos. Sometimes DJ's or bands play at these to advertise their availability. More often, though, you can get business cards at these events about DJ's and bands.

Some DJ's are part of large entertainment agencies or DJ businesses. Others are quite small one-person affairs. DJ agencies usually have lots of equipment, a vast musical library, and backup DJ's if something happens to the DJ you hired.

Smaller businesses may be able to give you more personal attention and may cost less. You will need to find out what kind of equipment they have and the size of their libraries. Also, you'll need to find out if there is backup if the DJ becomes ill. Try to avoid your cousin's teenage friend who's been spinning tunes at the local teen hangout. He wouldn't have the experience needed to handle the elegance of a formal wedding ceremony.

Choose three or four DJ's and make appointments to consult with them, just like you would for a band. Ask if the DJ has a recent video of a wedding to see how he interacts with the crowd. Remember, though, that every wedding is different and the DJ, if he's good at what he does, will individually tailor his routine to your wishes.

Ask for references and call them. Ask about how the DJ responded to unexpected events during the evening and how he got people up dancing. Find out how long the DJ has been in business and how many wedding ceremonies he has done. Does the DJ have liability insurance?

Find out what their normal wedding attire is. Usually the DJ wears a tuxedo. If the men in your wedding are wearing tuxedos, then the DJ definitely should wear one. If the men are wearing suits, then a good suit would be acceptable. Make sure that the DJ isn't ultra-casual.

The next thing to consider is the size and variety of the DJ's music collection. Bring a list of special songs when you meet with the DJ. Find out what medium his music collection is in. Most often it's CD's, although once in awhile you will find a DJ who also travels with a turntable and vinyl records. More and more DJs are turning to digital systems, meaning that their entire library is inside a computer that is programmable. Some DJ libraries can vary from 200 CD's to thousands. The average is about 1,000 CD's. No matter how many a DJ has, make sure that he has the variety or genre that you're looking for and the specific songs you want

The next consideration is the DJ's sound system. Ask him what it is and how big it is. Make sure that the system fits the ceremony site. You don't want to overpower your quests with too much sound. And, you want to make sure that the sound is clear and without distortion, especially if the DJ is providing the microphone for the wedding ceremony. Some standard DJ equipment consists of four speakers, two amplifiers, two CD players, and a microphone. Usually, it is a wireless one, although some DJ's prefer to use a wireless headset.

The DJ will need to set up before your guests arrive and do a sound check. Usually, this only takes thirty minutes. Have the church or facility manager dress the table well before the DJ arrives and locate it out of the way of the main ceremony activity.

Finally, ask what other engagements the DJ has for the day of your reception. You don't want to have him rush through your wedding ceremony just so he can make his next gig, and you don't want to find out he's stuck in traffic in Timbuktu and can't set up on time.

What is the DJ's fee and what's included? Find out if there is a cancellation policy and a backup plan.

When you have made your decision, put everything in writing in a detailed contract. Then, give the DJ a deposit. Usually, this is anywhere from 10% to 60% of the fee. You may then pay the final amount the day of the wedding and offer a tip at your discretion. It is a nice courtesy to offer the DJ food and beverages.

Please remember that a professional wedding DJ knows his job. If you decide you just don't want to pay for a professional, you may be able to delegate this task to a trusted person. You may have friends or relatives who have run sound for community theater groups, schools, or churches. You might even get very lucky and have a friend or relative who has worked in a radio station that still cues its own music. If there is a music tech school near you, post a notice for a music tech person to run your music for your wedding. Any of these people would have the most experience in handling music media and the equipment needed to play them at your wedding.

Make sure that the music you choose is in an easy form to play. Make a list of the tracks on the CDs or tapes you will be using. You may wish to record all of your selections onto a blank CD in the order you want them. Your music person will then just need to put in the CD and fade the music in and out.

Next, check out any audio equipment at the ceremony site. If there isn't any, ask whether your music person has a portable system with big enough speakers and would be willing to use it on the day of the wedding.

Church Organists and Soloists

When you book some churches, they will insist that you use their church organists or soloists. You may have no choice in a situation such as this but to use the organist and soloist provided. This usually means that the marriage ceremony is proscribed, with very little variation. You may not have very much choice in any aspect of your ceremony in this case, except to choose readings and music from an authorized booklet.

If the church organist and soloist are being offered as a courtesy, then you may graciously decline in favor of your own performers. Many churches have lists of many such wedding specialists and offer names to be helpful. There is no oughtness to their suggestions. Make sure you read the church's wedding booklet to find out just exactly what you can and cannot do in a wedding at that church.

Wedding Musician Options

There are lots of options for musicians for your wedding ceremony. You can use an organist or pianist to announce the bride's arrival or to underline the unity candle ceremony. You can opt for the lilting notes of harpists, flutists, and guitars. You can choose the romance of a chamber orchestra or the clear tones of a soprano or tenor soloist. You can also select Celtic groups or reggae musicians. The possibilities are endless.

How Much Music?

The number of songs you will need depends on the length of your ceremony, special moments that you want to highlight, and wedding style and theme. Commonly, weddings have two to three musical selections before the wedding and three to five during the ceremony. More music may be added if you have more going on in your wedding ceremony. You can also have as few as two.

These musical selections usually are found in the processional or entrance music and the recessional or exit music. Most often, this music is instrumental. The recessional is nearly always instrumental. After all, no soloist wants to finish a song to an empty house.

Additional songs can be added in other places. Before the processional, there often is music as your guests are being seated. This is called the prelude. These selections can be instrumental or vocal solos. Some couples add a song after the vows and rings, between readings, and/or during the lighting of the unity candle. For Christian services, there may also be hymns during the offertory and communion.

Choosing Music

Music for a religious wedding. Check with the church organist, music director, or church wedding coordinator to see what the church music policy is. Most Protestant churches use both secular and religious music at weddings. However, some churches, especially Catholic churches and some conservative evangelical churches, may insist that you only use liturgical music and no popular music at all. Although, many Catholic churches will allow classical and some secular music during the prelude, which is usually fifteen minutes before the wedding mass. Similarly, many Orthodox Jewish rabbis want traditional musical selections, whereas many Conservative and Reform rabbis will permit popular and classical music in weddings.

Length. When you have a list of possible songs for the different parts of your ceremony, check the length of each selection. Make sure that each song is the right length for the intended activity. For a processional song, you will need a piece of music that will take you down the aisle without having to stand in front of your guests waiting for the song to finish. You can fudge on this if you are using instrumental music. Either the recorded music can be slowly faded out or a skilled musician will take the cue and slowly end the song.

Examples of Song Lengths

Songs between readings: 2-3 minutes
Songs after the exchange of vows and rings: 2-3 minutes
Songs during the unity candle lighting: 1-2 minutes
Hymns for offertory: 2-3 minutes
Hymns for communion: 5-7 minutes or two shorter pieces.

Music Suggestions

Prelude Music. As your guests arrive, have some music that
will set the mood for the ceremony. Prelude music, starting
about thirty minutes before the wedding, should be light and
played at a low volume. This is a good time for a soloist to
sing a few romantic songs or for an ethnic group to perform
a few selections appropriate to your wedding theme.

Prelude Music Selections

Sophisticated.
Violin Concerto #8–Vilvaldi
Rondo–Mozart
Air (from The Water Music)–Handel
Concerto #1 (from The Four Seasons, Spring)–Vivaldi
Moonlight Sonata–Beethoven
Nocturne in E-Flat–Mozart
The Immigrant (love theme)–Godfather soundtrack
Clare de Lune–Debussy
Dance of the Blessed Spirits - Gluck

Festive/Joyous
Brandenberg Concerto #2–Bach
Hornpipe in D (from The Water Music)–Handel
Rondo for Flute and Orchestra–Mozart

Romantic
One Hand, One Heart (from West Side Story)–Sonheim/Bernstein
All I Ask of You (from Phantom of the Opera)- Webber
Swan Lake–Tchaikovsky
Lough Erin Shores–The Corrs
Only Time–Enya
I Will Be Here–Steven Curtis Chapman
Forever in Love- Kenny G
Waltz (from Sleeping Beauty)–Tchaikovsky
For the Love of a Princess–Braveheart soundtrack
My Heart Will Go On–Celine Dion

Religious
Jesu, Joy of Man's Desiring–Bach
Largo (from Xerxes)–Handel
God is My Shepherd–Antoni Dvorak

Processional. Processional music comes in two parts. One is for the entrance of the wedding party, led by the groomsmen, the bridesmaids, the maid/matron of honor, the ring bearer, and the flower girl. The other is the ta-da moment when the bride appears and the guests rise to welcome her entrance. The bride's musical selection should be different enough from the bridesmaids' song so that the guests will know that the bride is coming. Both songs should have a rhythm that is easy to walk to. If you select the same piece of music for both entrances, make sure that the bride's music is much louder.

Processional Song Selections

Wedding Party Entrance
Canon in D Major–Pachelbel
Air on a G String–Bach
A Day Without Rain - Enya
Forrest Gump Suite–Forrest Gump soundtrack
Fields of Gold–Sting
Maid Marion–Robin Hood: Prince of Thieves soundtrack
Heart of a King–Man in the Iron Mask soundtrack
Erev Ba–Shoshana Damari

Bride's Entrance
Bridal Chorus (from Lohengrin)–Wagner
Arrival of the Queen of Sheeba–Handel
Suite in D Major (Trumpet Voluntary)–Clark
Wedding March (from Lohengrin)–Wagner

Processional Love Songs
From This Moment–Shania Twain & Bryan White
Only time–Enya
The Wedding Song–Kenny G
At Last–Etta James
Ready for Love–India Arie
Give Me Forever, I Do–John Tesh
We Must Be in Love–Pure Soul
True Love–Bing Crosby
More–Andy Williams

Ceremony Music. Musical selections for the ceremony are usually romantic songs.

Ceremony Song Selections

Love Songs

I Swear–J. M. Montgomery
Have I Told You Lately–Rod Stewart or Van Morrison
Everything I Do–Bryan Adams
Unforgettable–Nat King Cole
Wind Beneath My Wings–Bette Midler
Unchained Melody–The Righteous Brothers
Power of Love–Celine Dion
What a Wonderful World–Louis Armstrong
Wonderful Tonight–Eric Clapton
I Love the Way You Love Me–J. M. Montgomery
Endless Love–Mariah Carey and Luther Vandross
When a Man Loves a Woman–Percy Sledge or Michael Bolton
Always and Forever–Luther Vandross
Can't Help Falling in Love–Elvis Presley
True Companion–Marc Cohen
Beautiful in My Eyes–Joshua Kadison
Beautiful–Gordon Lightfoot
Your Love Amazes Me–John Berry

Unity Candle Music

Grow Old with Me–Shania Twain and Bryan White
One Hand, One Heart (from West Side Story)
Flesh of My Flesh–Leon Patillo
Me and You–Kenny Chesney
I Believe in You and Me–Whitney Houston
When I Said I Do–Clint Black and Lisa Hartman-Black
Household of Faith–Steve and Anne Paynter
Give Me Forever, I Do–John Tesh
When You Say Nothing at All–Allison Kraus
You Light Up My Life–Leann Rimes

Circle of Life–Lion King soundtrack
I'll Always Be Right There–Bryan Adams
Love of My Life–Sammy Kershaw
Once in a Lifetime Love–Alan Jackson
True Companion–Marc Cohn
Watermark - Enya

Wedding Blessing
Forever Young–Bob Dylan

Recessional. The recessional begins as soon as the couple shares the bridal kiss or the celebrant introduces the couple as husband and wife. The selections should be joyful and celebratory.

Recessional Song Selections

Ode to Joy (from 9th Symphony)–Beethoven
Wedding March (from Midsummer Night's Dream)–Mendelssohn
Star Wars (main title)–John Williams
Everlasting Love–Natalie Cole
What a Wonderful World–Louis Armstrong
At the Beginning–Anastasia soundtrack
Cowboy Take Me Away–Dixie Chicks
All I Need Is Love–Beatles
Hawaiian Wedding Song–Elvis Presley
Signed, Sealed, Delivered–Stevie Wonder
Book of Days–Enya
Wrapped Up in You–Garth Brooks
Hooked on a Feeling–Blue Swede

Postlude. This is very joyful music and forms a backdrop for a receiving line or for the guests to leave.

Postlude Music Selections

Overture (from Music for the Royal Fireworks)–Handel
Rondeau–Mouret
Le Rejouissance (from Music for the Royal Fireworks)–Handel
Trumpet Tune and Air–Purcell
Suite in F Major–Handel

Devotional Songs. Religious or devotional music doesn't necessarily have to be hymns. Much of the new contemporary gospel music is appropriate for weddings. Among the performers to check out are Amy Grant, Twila Paris, and Michael W. Smith.

Songs for Christian Weddings

You Dream of Me–Michael W. Smith
Faithful Friend–Twila Paris
Fall in Love Again–Mark Schultz
Finally–Gary Chapman
Flesh of My Flesh–Leon Patillo
Holding On to You–Servant
Household of Faith–Steve Green
I Do (Promise to Love You)–Phil and Brenda Nicholas
I Found Myself in You–Clay Crosse
I Found Love–Geoff Moore and the Distance
I Will Be Here for You–Michael W. Smith
I Will Never Go–Twila Paris
Jesus in Your Eyes–Julie Miller
Love–Petra
Love Has a Hold on Me–Amy Grant
The Love I Found in You–Steve Camp
Love Moves in Mysterious Ways–Michael English
Lover of My Soul–Amy Grant
One at Heart–Servant
The One I've Been Waiting For–Out of the Grey
Only God Could Love You More–Kelly Nelon Thompson
Perfect Union–Matthew Ward
Since I Found You–Matthew Ward
Still in Love–East to West
Till the End of time–Steve Green
T Keep Love Alive–Out of the Grey
Together as One–Stryper
True Companion–Marc Cohn
True Friend–Twila Paris
Take My Hand–Between Thieves
There Will Never Be Another–Amy Grant
The Two of You–Phil Keaggy
Two Trusting Jesus–Mark Heard

Walk Forever by My Side–The Alarm
The Wedding–Michael Card
Wedding Prayer–Glenn Kaiser
Wedding Song (There Is Love)–Noel Paul Stookey
What a Wonder You Are–Phil Keaggy
When the Love Is Right–Tourniquet
You and I–Guardian
Your Love–Guardian
You're a Gift from God–Kenny Marks

Rehearsals

If you will be working with live musicians and soloists, you may decide to arrange a meeting with them at the ceremony site. This doesn't necessarily need to be done on your official wedding rehearsal night. By meeting with them privately, you will allow them to look at the space and find out where they will be placed during the ceremony. They will also be able to test the acoustics and possibly try out sound equipment or instruments in the space.

If it isn't possible to get into the ceremony site before the wedding, still arrange a meeting with your musicians and soloists. Ask them to play the selections you have asked them to do. Please remember that musical artists often interpret songs. Your hired musicians and soloists may not sound like what you heard on studio-tweaked recordings by your favorite artists on the radio. There will be differences in tempo and phrasing. After all, you didn't hire Celine Deon or George Strait to sing at your wedding. If you did your homework and listened to your musicians before hiring them, there won't be any big surprises.

CHAPTER FIFTEEN

CREATING PERMANENT MEMORIES

Choosing a Photographer

Selecting the right person to create permanent memories of your wedding day is an important step. If you hire someone who doesn't follow your wishes, you may end up with pictures of people and scenes you don't want or strange art photos that never show a person's face clearly. How do you find that perfect photographer?

First, you ask your friends, your co-workers, and your relatives who did their wedding photography. If two or three names keep popping up, chances are you have found someone whose work is good. But is it your style?

Start by phoning the studios you've uncovered. Ask a lot of preliminary questions before you make an appointment to see the photographer's work. Ask about availability for your wedding date. If there is more than one photographer at a studio, find out who would be doing your wedding. Get a rough, ballpark estimate of costs and what is generally included. Discuss the studio's take on wedding photography. Do they do one style or is a variety available? What do they think of photojournalism, formal portraits, candid shots, or group photos? If you like what you hear, make an appointment to meet the photographer who would be available to work your wedding and see his work.

Decide who should come to this meeting. Some couples prefer to meet the photographer alone in order to have any distractions. Others want to include your parents or your best man and maid/matron of honor. These couples want as much input as they can get in making this very important decision.

At the meeting, pay special attention to how the photographer makes you feel. Does the photographer try to get to know you? Are you asked about what you want? Do you feel comfortable with this person?

Next, ask to see samples of the photographer's work. If there are photos that you really like, ask the photographer if you might call the couple in the photos for a personal reference. Though the pictures might be wonderful, if the couple didn't like working with the photographer, it is just as much a negative as a poor picture. Talking with the bridal couple in the photos verifies that the photos were taken by the photographer you talked with.

Sometimes, photo studios have a stable of photographers and will often show prospective clients their sample book, which contains work by all of their artists. Unless, you can verify who took what photo, you would never know. Make sure that the photo samples you look at come from the photographer who will be on site to photograph your wedding.

Though most couples' main concern is price, the size of the pictures, and how many that they will get, there are other factors to consider. These concern the photographer's philosophy surrounding the whole picture-taking process. Ask about how the photographer feels about the bride and groom not wanting to see each other before the ceremony. How will the photographer take formal shots? Will it be after the ceremony? Does the photographer have a special approach for each wedding? How much time does the photographer plan to spend with the couple on their wedding day? Are there overtime charges? Who and what will be photographed? What can the bridal couple do to help the photographer do his best?

Digital photography poses a few extra questions. Ask the photographer or photo studio if they will edit and color correct the digital images before they are printed. Is it the photographer or someone working with the photo studio who does this work? Do they hire the work out to a number of individuals? It is crucial to find these answers because two different studios can edit the same image and print very different photos.

After you have had time to think over the responses to these questions, make another appointment and ask to see photos from a complete wedding. Evaluate what you see. Do you think the photographer has captured the personality of the important people in the pictures? Do you see feelings in the photos or just stiff, posed shots?

Next, ask a Hollywood question. What are the best features of the bride and groom? What is my best side? What can the photographer do to show off the wedding party to its best advantage? Has the photographer already noticed any mannerisms or expressions that could be enhanced or avoided in photos?

Finally, ask about the experience and qualifications the photographer has. Where did the photographer train? How many years has the photographer been in business? Where and when was the photographer's last technique updated? What is the process for selecting photos—proofs? slides? video? How much time will the photographer need for preparation of the couples' selections and for the final photos? How much for duplicates? Don't forget to ask about all day coverage and travel fees. Ask about cancellations and refunds. Find out what the payment process is.

Ask about black and white photography. Though color film is readily available, many couples are opting for the sophistication of black and white film. Ask if there is an extra fee for black and white. Ask whether the photographer also does hand coloring or digital coloring for black and white and digital color separation. What are the fees for each?

Necessary Photos

The photo session begins with the bride, then the bride and groom. The next photos usually follow this sequence: the bride and groom with the bride's family, the bride and groom with the groom's family, the groom with his parents, the bride and groom with any grandparents, and, finally, the wedding party. This order of photos allows both families to mingle with their guests as soon as possible.

Optional Photos

Weddings are occasions that families and old friends get together and renew their ties. Capturing their presence in photographs at your wedding will preserve these memories for them as well as reminding you that it was the happy occasion of your marriage that brought these folks together again. If you are inviting aunts and uncles, have a photo taken of them with your parents as a reunion photo, with you in the center, or just them in a group. If you have a group of high school friends, camp friends, fraternity or sorority members, co-workers, or godparents, take photographs of them grouped together. You can do the same with all of your siblings and their spouses and children or all of your cousins.

These photos aren't usually taken by professional photographers though they would be happy to do so. Make a list of those groups that you would like to have photographed. Ask your photographer to take some extra time to photograph these people as well. They will then shoot these folks when your formal wedding photos are taken, either before the ceremony or immediately afterward. Make sure that you notify these people that they will have their photos taken and to be available when the photographer sets up to do your formal shots. This will save you from having to herd them into the ceremony site when they've already headed for the bar and the buffet table.

Journalistic Style

There is a new trend in wedding photography that is taking off. Beginning almost thirty years ago by a few artistic photographers who thought it would be a creative way to capture a wedding, photographers have begun to create photojournalistic essays of wedding celebrations. Taken mainly in black and white, though color is still popular, these photographers follow the bride and groom throughout their wedding day, capturing candid moments. Taken together, these photos become an intimate portrait of the bridal couple. Think of it as Life magazine capturing your wedding.

Many photographers who do photojournalistic style will still take formal group shots before or after the ceremony. But, you will have to ask them to do it.

Budget

As you plan to capture you wedding day memories, keep in mind that, generally, costs for photography and/or videography composes 8% of the entire wedding budget. For a $25,000 wedding, that amounts to $2,000. If your wedding budget is much smaller, you will need to trim costs here. Don't skimp on quality, though. You may want to cut down on the number of prints you receive or trim the number of shots or cut the time the photographer will work.

Choosing a Videographer

Basically, a videographer creates a video documentary of your wedding. It can just be the wedding ceremony from start to finish or it can cover the entire day with getting ready, interviews with the couple and the wedding party, the wedding itself, the reception, and going away. The video can be in color or black and white. There are also different filming techniques that the videographer can use.

The bridal couple should look at previous work by the videographer and discuss different options. Fees generally depend on the amount of time the videographer spends shooting your video and editing the results.

Ask the usual business questions and some specific about the videography business. How much experience does the videographer have? Who will be videotaping your wedding? How many cameras will be used? Will there be other personnel at the wedding as well? What kind of lighting will be used? What kind and how many microphones will be used? How is the editing done? Does the videographer offer special effects? Can the videographer convert the video to DVD? How disruptive will the videographer be to your wedding day events? What do the fees cover? How long will the footage be kept on file?

Always ask to see a copy of the videographer's standard contract. Ask how your contract will differ.

Video Extras

There are many creative additions that a skilled videographer can use to enhance your wedding video. One popular trend is to include childhood pictures of you and your groom and other candid shots taken during your courtship. These are put together in a montage at the beginning of the video that creates the background for the wedding footage. Couples often give the videographer a list of their favorite songs or choose from a list that the videographer provides to underline these special photos.

Sometimes, couples ask for a short version video along with the longer footage. This shorter piece is heavily edited, but it will be one that you and your friends will be willing to watch over and over again. The longer version becomes an archive for your family. If this extended version is burned to DVD, it will last much longer.

Another idea is showing a photomontage at your rehearsal dinner or at the reception. It is put together much like the background footage used in the wedding video. Personal musical choices also provide the soundtrack. Many couples also have a photomontage created for important anniversaries.

A more ambitious undertaking is a documentary of your wedding. It isn't just the wedding day and all of the activities that entails. It is a film of the making of your wedding, from the planning, the dress fittings, the trip to the beauty salon for your hair, meetings with the caterer, and even the making of your wedding cake. This could be filmed by friends or the videographer and then edited by a professional.

Finally, find out if your videographer can upload your shortened wedding video or post photos on the Internet. Often videographers are digital and computer gurus. They may be able to even stream the video on your website.

Caveats for Religious Spaces

Churches, synagogues, and shrines are sacred places. Photography should be tasteful, and the photographer should be unobtrusive, only observing and recording. The use of studio equipment such as screens, umbrella lighting, etc. may not be permitted inside the sanctuary of the church (the main church area). In Catholic churches, photographers and videographers are not permitted on the raised altar area (also called the sanctuary), nor on its steps or the area in front of the first pew. The photographer should not be in front of the altar, the musicians, or the lectern. Often, they must shoot from the side or rear of the church. They cannot position photographic equipment or themselves in the center aisle facing the procession. Some churches, restrict the photographer to a pew, halfway back in the church. Photographers also are not permitted to slow or stop the processional or any other part of the liturgy. Flash may be restricted during the ceremony but permitted during the processional and recessional. In all cases, furnishings belonging to the religious space should not be moved.

Wedding photos can be taken before the ceremony or immediately afterward. If they are done afterward, make sure those involved know to gather immediately after the recessional. Also, because your time will be limited, usually 30 to 45 minutes after the end of the ceremony, you should probably dispense with a receiving line at the church. In fact, if you read our companion book, *The Ul-*

timate Wedding Reception Book, you will note that we recommend that receiving lines be eliminated both at the church and at the reception. You will still be able to greet your guests if you follow our innovative order for the reception.

In Catholic churches, find out what time Confession starts and the next Mass is. You will not be permitted to finish your photography once Confession begins.

Informal photographs taken by family and friends are often not permitted during the ceremony in many churches because it is disruptive. Place a notice in the wedding program saying that photography is not permitted during the ceremony.

Make sure that the photographer meets with the celebrant a half hour to fifteen minutes before the ceremony to see if the celebrant has any last minute instructions.

Photography Tips

If your reception is at another location, try not to schedule it too close to the end of the ceremony if you are doing photos after the wedding service. If your photography session will be 45 minutes to an hour and you have a half hour commute to the reception, you will need to also figure in time for the photographer to break down the equipment and set it up at the reception site. Many people in this circumstance allow a two-hour gap between the ceremony and the reception. If the reception is in the same facility, an hour gap is fine. You may want to open the bar at your reception a half hour early to accommodate your guests.

If you have your photos taken before the ceremony or you only have a couple of photos done after the ceremony, then you can schedule your reception much closer to the end of the ceremony.

Also, if your photos will be taken in the ceremony site before the wedding, make sure that your florist delivers all of the wedding ceremony flowers early enough so that they will be in place for the photos. You don't want to have your wedding portrait taken without your bouquet.

In addition, have a backup location in mind if you are having your photos taken outdoors. Make sure that an indoor space will be available for that purpose on your wedding day.

Finally, select someone to act as a photo-coordinator to help the photographer. What this person does is gather the family members together for their photos at the appointed time. Though the photographer may be given a list of people to photograph, unless someone points out who these people are, the photographer won't know who to shoot. The photo-coordinator can help point the photographer in the right direction. It is also a good idea to have the photo-coordinator and the photographer visit the ceremony and reception sites before the wedding day. The photographer will benefit from such a preview of the space so that he can make lighting decisions and look for the best places within the space to take photos. This is critical for unusual locations. A museum or park will offer very different photo opportunities and restrictions than a church.

CHAPTER SIXTEEN

GETTING TO THE CHURCH (AND RECEPTION) ON TIME

Usually, the bride and her bridesmaids drive to the ceremony site where they dress for the wedding. Some reception sites will also allow you to come in early to dress and will secure your belongings so that you can then be picked up by a limousine for the wedding ceremony. If the reception is at a hotel, some brides rent a room to dress in. One or more of the bridesmaids usually stays there after the reception.

The best man drives the groom to the ceremony location, while the groomsmen get there on their own. After the wedding, either the best man or a professional limo driver gets the bride and groom to the reception. And, the bride and groom either take a limo to the airport or get in the groom's car and drive away.

Unusual Ways to Get There

The perfect getaway vehicle is really up to your individual taste and your wallet. Some couples like to ride off in a horse-drawn buggy. Some want to drift off in a brightly colored, hot air balloon. You can drive into the sunset in elegant sedan cars, vintage cars, or Rolls Royces. Some limo companies and car rental companies often have sports cars and luxury cars for rent. You'll need a trusted friend or relative to act as driver, but it could be a romantic and less expensive option to a limo. You could also arrive in a dune buggy, on a tractor, on horseback, or astride a Haley Davidson Blackhawk. Most couples just want to speed away in any available vehicle

Please remember if you want to decorate someone's wedding car, what you put on the finish might not come off. Putting rocks in the hub cabs is harmless and so is tying shoes or tin cans to the rear bumper. But the shoes or tin cans will have to be removed if the couple goes any distance. Also, make sure the car's windshield is left alone and nothing is put in the gas tank. We want the bridal couple to have a fun sendoff, and we want them to reach their wedding hotel safely and with no added expenses.

Finding a Limousine Service

Ask recently married friends and relatives what limousine service they have used. Even ask your wedding vendors, especially your caterer or floral designer for recommendations. They have probably worked with many of the limousine services in your town and would definitely know the best ones.

Once you have compiled a short list of businesses, call and compare prices. The national average for a limo is $50 an hour with a built-in 15% tip. Most limos will need to be reserved at least six months in advance, so make your plans early.

Visit each limo service and look at the vehicles they have available. Ask about make and model and whether their older vehicles are in good condition. Find out the seating capacity of each vehicle you are interested in. Be very clear in ordering. For example, you don't want a 6-passenger stretch limo to pull up when you needed an 8-passenger one.

Look for other colors besides white. Sometimes, a black or silver limo will cost as much as 10% less. Also, find out if the limo services have vintage, classic, and luxury cars for rent, complete with drivers. These can also be less expensive than a limo.

Look for extras thrown into wedding packages. Sometimes, you can get a free bottle of champagne or a decorated limo with a personalized Just Married sign.

Ask about how the fees are determined. Are they based on time or distance or both? Do they have a three-hour minimum? Do they have a pick up and drop off service? Can you book the limo and driver for all day? What is their tipping policy? Ask about discounts for booking multiple cars?

Also, find out what the limo driver will be wearing. His degree of formality should match your wedding style.

When you've found what you want, don't rush to sign the contract until you've had a chance to check out the company's reference. If everything is satisfactory, then get everything is in writing, including the full price, the deposit, any cancellation policies, and extras. Give the limo service directions to all of the locations where the limo will pick you up and drop you off. You don't want to be giving the driver directions all day from the back seat or getting frustrated because you don't know if the drive will get lost.

Confirm all of the details about a week before the wedding. It's also a good idea to call the limo company a day or two before the wedding to make sure there are no surprises.

Getting In and Out of the Limo without Falling on Your Face

Bridal gowns often are made of yards and yards of fabric. You don't want to wrinkle the gown too much as you crowd into a compact car. Large limos keep the fabric crisp and allow the bride to breathe a bit better.

But how do you get in and out of a vehicle without getting tangled in all that material? First, the limo driver should open the door for you as you gather as much of your skirt as you can and push it to the front of your body. One of your bridesmaids should hold onto your train and veil, and another should hold your bridal bouquet. Turn your back to the door opening, bend at the waist, and gently lower yourself into the seat. Straighten out your upper body and turn, bringing your train with you. Move your feet into the car and adjust your skirt and bring your train over your lap. This minimizes wrinkles and keeps you from getting your heels caught in the material as you try to stand.

Just lean back and relax. Don't slide over or move from this position. If you do, you'll wrinkle someplace important. Whoever else is riding with you should enter from the left side door.

Have one of your bridesmaids pass your flowers to you, but don't rest them on your dress. Lay them on the seat next to you or in front of you.

When you get to your destination, the driver should pull up so that your door is next to the curb. Be patient and stay put until the driver opens the door and your bridesmaids are ready to help you with your train and flowers. The bride always is the last person to leave the limo anyway.

Hand the train to your bridesmaid. Turn your feet and body toward the curb. Put your feet on the ground and stick your head out. Let the driver or someone take your elbow and help you out. Once on your feet, release your dress and have your bridesmaid let go of your train. Let everything fall into place, adjusting what you need to. Have your bridesmaid get your flowers from the limo for you, and you're all set.

CHAPTER SEVENTEEN

FINISHING TOUCHES

Decorating the Ceremony Site

Check with the ceremony site about what are appropriate decorations for your wedding. If you are having the ceremony in a church or synagogue, there may be some restrictions about where to place decorations, including flowers, pew decorations, and even aisle runners.

While flowers are the main wedding decorations, many couples will opt to use banners, bunting, balloons, or other decorative items that are in keeping with their wedding theme at their ceremony site. Again, make sure that whatever you want to bring into the space is appropriate. Many churches only want flowers inside their buildings.

Some ceremony sites don't want anything pinned, stapled, nailed, or glued to the building or furniture. That is only common courtesy. After all, you wouldn't want someone to come into your home and start nailing things to your entertainment center or your Queen Anne chairs.

Rice and Other Customs

Many churches and other public buildings do not permit throwing rice, birdseed, or confetti on their premises, even outside. That makes sense because these items are difficult to clean up.

Some facilities will permit other customs, though many churches, especially Catholic churches, do not want these customs inside or outside the church. Some couples release helium filled balloons in their wedding colors. Other couples release butterflies or doves. Though the release of living things is very romantic, it can be an environmental problem, especially if the species is not native nor has been adapted to a specific ecosystem. That beautiful dove you released into the city as a symbol of your pure love may end up contributing to urban blight or being zapped by pigeon control measures in your city. So, think before you involve living creatures in your wedding.

Guests are sometimes given little bottles of bubbles to greet the bride and groom as they leave the ceremony location. Though this is a really lovely idea, again, clean up can be a problem. And, a lot of churches don't permit this.

Always check with the ceremony venue before adding any of these wedding activities.

Wedding Favors for Guests

Many people like to take something away as a souvenir of your wedding. Usually, it is something they receive at the reception. These items can be very inexpensive, but highly personal. Some can be contracted for from custom advertising companies. Just as you might order pencils or mugs for your company, you can order custom items for your wedding, in addition to keepsake napkins with your name and wedding date. A good general rule for cost is to calculate the amount per person you are spending on food and beverages (not including the cake). Then take 9% to 12% of that figure to determine how much per person you can spend on favors or other table decorations.

You can place little bottles of jam or cider on the tables if you are having a country wedding. You can put framed photos of the bride and groom on each table and give them to whoever is seated there. You can display bird's nests, doves, bells, seashell soaps, seeds and seedlings or other potted plants, dried herbs or flowers, Christmas decorations for a winter wedding, floating candles, Victorian sachets, miniature sports equipment, toy cars, toy horses or other animals, bubbles, and Hershey's kisses. You can also put out personalized bookmarks, notepads, magnets, chocolate roses, or personalized chocolate bars. All of these items can be customized with the wedding couple's name and wedding date on them.

CHAPTER EIGHTEEN

RESOURCES

BOOKS

General

Henry S. Basayne and Linda R. Janowitz
Weddings: The Magic of Creating Your Own Ceremony

Bill Cox with Janie Franz
The Ultimate Wedding Reception Book
The Ultimate Wedding Workbook (coming soon)

Sharon Dlugosch
Wedding Plans: 50 Unique Themes for the Wedding of Your Dreams.

Denise Fields
Far and Away Weddings: Secrets to Planning a Long-Distance Wedding.

Barbara Metrick
I Do: A Guide to Creating Your Own Unique Wedding Ceremony

Cindy Moore and Tricia Windom, with Martha Giddens Nesbit
Planning a Wedding with Divorced Parents.

Jane Ross-Macdonald
Alternative Weddings: An Essential Guide for Creating Your Own Ceremony

Diane Warner
Beautiful Wedding Decorations & Gifts on a Small Budget. Picture-Perfect Worry-Free Weddings: 72 Destinations & Venues.

Speeches and Toasts

John Bowden
Making a Wedding Speech: How to Prepare and Deliver a Confident and Memorable Address.

Barbara Jeffery
Wedding Speeches and Toasts.

Eleanor Munro
Wedding Readings: Centuries of Writing and Rituals on Love and Marriage

Carley Roney
The Knot Guide to Wedding Words and Music: Vows, Traditions, Rituals, Music, Dances, Speeches and Toasts

Diane Warner
Diane Warner's Complete Book of Wedding Toasts (Hundreds of Ways to Say "Congratulations!

Diane Warner's Complete Book of Wedding Vows: Hundreds of Ways to Say I Do

Marty Younkin and Carol Sage (editors)
A Wedding Ceremony to Remember: Perfect Words for the Perfect Wedding

Religious, Theme, and Cultural Weddings

Kwabena F. Ashanti
African Royal Wedding and Marriage Ceremony: A Guide

Anita Diamant
The New Jewish Wedding

Andy Langford
Christian Weddings: Resources to Make Your Ceremony Unique

Devon A. Lerner
Celebrating Interfaith Marriages: Creating Your Jewish/ Christian Ceremony

Lisl M. Spangenberg
Timeless Traditions: How to Blend Wedding Customs from Around the World into Your Own Wedding Ceremony

Etiquette

Pamela A. Piljac
Bride's Thank You Guide: Thank-You Writing Made Easy

Destination Wedding Sources

Amusement Park Wedding Contacts

Disney World's Fairy Tale Weddings
Orlando FL
(407) 828-3400
www.disney.go.com

Disneyland's Fairy Tale Weddings
Anaheim CA
(714) 956-6527
www.disney.go.com

SeaWorld
Orlando Fl
(407) 363-2273
www.seaworld.com

Busch Gardens
Tampa FL
(813) 987-5209
www.buschgardens.com

Knotts Berry Farm
Buena Park CA
(714) 243-2028
www.knots.com/Catering/catering.htm

Dollywood
Pigeon Forge TN
(423) 428-9488
www.dollywood.com

Dutch Wonderland
E. Lancaster PA
(717) 534-4900

www.dutchwonderland.com

Hershey Chocolate World
Hershey PA
(717) 534-4900
www.hersheys.com/chocworld

Six Flags Over Texas
Arlington TX
(817) 640-8900
www.sixflags.com

Bermuda Weddings

Bermuda Wedding Associates Broadway House 1 Crow Lane
Pembroke, HM 19 Bermuda Mailing Address: PO Box CR 228
Hamilton Parish CR BX Bermuda
Tel: 441-293-4033 Fax: 441-292-3186 email: *shamill@ibl.bm*

Cruise Ship Weddings

A Wedding For You, Inc. 10860 Southwest 38th Drive
Davie, FL 33328-1328 US (954) 472-0320 or (800) 929-4198
Fax (954) 473-9932

Other

Mall of America, Chapel of Love
Minneapolis MN
(800) 299-LOVE
www.mlonda@chapeloflove.com

Unique Wedding Accessories

Barefeet.4U
Unique, elegant crystal and pearl footwear
www.barefeet4u.com

Island Wedding Shop
Island themed wedding accessories
www.islandweddingshop.com

Caribbean Wraps International
Wedding sarongs
www.allyoutowear.com